T0053689

"*Walk in Balance* is a powerful collection of wisdom for the ages. In this book, Lynn Andrews has masterfully recapitulated the knowledge she has gained from many masters. If you follow the daily meditations, this book becomes a great tool of inspiration and empowerment. If you have a question, just open the book and read a passage. This book serves as a personal oracle as well. I truly believe that this is a most inspirational and practical guide to inner personal growth and development."

—**Roger Cantu**, author of *Powerful Mental Development* and director of the Los Angeles Meditation Center

"[*Tree of Dreams,*] . . . is right on time as always Lynn! It is awesome! I celebrate your Medicine gifts and this book brings them to us up front and personal. We are moving into the fifth world and people are realizing that they are different and that a maturing is happening for all ages. Your book is the heart of all this and will take us through the final transition. Your magic is water to our parched souls, and your clarity brings it to each of us on a personal level, and we are liberated with your guidance. No one does it better Beloved Sister."

—**Pa'Ris'Ha-T'Sali'gi**, Eastern Band Cherokee heritage, one of thirteen Grandmothers with Elders Without Borders that is organized by William Commanda, Algonquin elder, which consists of thirteen appointed Grandfathers and thirteen Grandmothers

"For me, Lynn has been a role model of the highest order. Her words and actions gave me permission and confidence to create a life led by Spirit and passion. She is the teacher's teacher: powerful, compassionate, open, intuitive, shamanic, wise, funny, and her teachings are cradled in Oneness. There would be no way I could express how grateful I am for the energy she has transmitted to free women and all living beings to help us soar. She is a treasure and a trailblazer. I feel so blessed to experience her consciousness and courage."

—Carol Simone

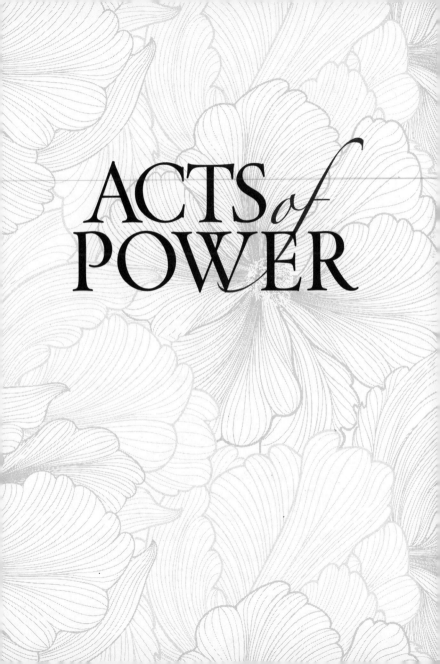

ACTS *of* POWER

ALSO BY LYNN ANDREWS

Medicine Woman

Spirit Woman / Flight of the Seventh Moon

Jaguar Woman

Star Woman

Crystal Woman

Windhorse Woman

The Woman of Wyrrd

Shakkai

Woman at the Edge of Two Worlds

Dark Sister

Love and Power

Tree of Dreams

Walk in Balance

Walk in Spirit

Writing Spirit

Coming Full Circle

Annie and the Butterfly Tree

Sacred Vision Oracle Cards

The Power Deck (Cards of Wisdom)

The Mask of Power Workbook & Journal

Teachings Around the Sacred Wheel Workbook

Woman at the Edge of Two Worlds Workbook

Love & Power Journal

Lynn V. Andrews

ACTS of POWER

Daily Teachings for Inspired Living

Artwork by Ursula Freer

BEYOND WORDS
Portland, Oregon

BEYOND WORDS

1750 S.W. Skyline Blvd., Suite 20
Portland, Oregon 97221-2543
503-531-8700 / 503-531-8773 fax
www.beyondword.com

First Beyond Words hardcover edition January 2022

BEYOND WORDS PUBLISHING is an imprint of Simon & Schuster Inc., and the Beyond Words logo is a registered trademark of Beyond Words Publishing, Inc.

For information about special discounts for bulk purchases, please contact Beyond Words Special Sales at 503-531-8700 or specialsales@beyondword.com.

Managing Editor: Lindsay S. Easterbrooks-Brown
Editor: Kathryn Duckworth
Proofreader: Madison Schultz
Interior design: Devon Smith
Cover design: Sue Denniston and Devon Smith
Cover artwork: Ursula Freer, UrsulaFreer.com
Composition: William H. Brunson Typography Services

Manufactured in Canada

10 9 8 7 6 5 4 3 2 1

Library of Congress Cataloging-in-Publication Data:

Names: Andrews, Lynn V., author.
Title: Acts of power : daily teachings for inspired living / Lynn V.
  Andrews.
Description: First Beyond Words hardcover edition. | Portland, OR : Beyond
  Words, 2022.
Identifiers: LCCN 2021032941 (print) | LCCN 2021032942 (ebook) | ISBN
  9781582708614 (hardback) | ISBN 9781582708621 (ebook)
Subjects: LCSH: Self-actualization (Psychology) | Mind and body.
Classification: LCC BF637.S4 A623 2022 (print) | LCC BF637.S4 (ebook) |
  DDC 158.1—dc23
LC record available at https://lccn.loc.gov/2021032941
LC ebook record available at https://lccn.loc.gov/2021032942

The corporate mission of Beyond Words Publishing, Inc.: *Inspire to Integrity*

CONTENTS

INTRODUCTION

Each of these daily messages are from my heart to yours. I hope you will join together with me and celebrate the magnificent journey of your very gifted life.

These inspirations are there for you when you need power. They will comfort you when you are in grief and help you sing in praise when you feel joy. They will inspire you if you already include the practice of prayer in your life and they will teach you how to contemplate simply and experientially if you have never learned. In a world filled with by rote endeavor, we so often perform the rituals of everyday life almost without thought. This is like driving down the freeway oblivious of the magnificent mountains and the diaphanous clouds above us. Because of our focus on our destination, we forget that life is a process and this moment is all that we will ever have. Sitting in the center of your own truth can bring you bliss and comfort. You are alive and aware and conscious now. Inspiration allows you to establish contact with the moment. It helps you travel the bridge between the physical world and the world of sacred vision. With prayer you can change your life.

Why is it important to have a new point of view for the day? It is a powerful heartfelt way of attracting the best aspects of creation to yourself. When you read something of beauty you then think thoughts that maybe you have forgotten about or have never known before. It helps you to find the embodiment of your heart and soul. You are a person in search of higher consciousness and awareness. These daily inspirations are sacred blessings.

As a twenty-first century shaman, I live an everyday life in the Western world but my teachers are native women from around the world. The inspirations in this book help you to balance the incredible stress of our current life with the ecstasy of wisdom and understanding that have been part of so many native cultures throughout history. They include blessings for all the seasons of the year and for the seasons of the soul. The difficulties and joys that the soul encounters in life are often mysterious and challenging. It has always helped me to find beautiful paragraphs, sentences, ideas and thoughts from other people of power. It is difficult in this twenty-first century with a foot in spirit and a foot in the physical world. Often times the only bridge between these two worlds is prayer and contemplation. Without inspirations and prayer, we may lose the world that we know forever. My beautiful teachers tell me with meditation and thoughtfulness we can transform the negative state of our societies and bring Mother Earth back into balance. It is in this spirit that I offer the affirmations and presentations of thought within this book. Every day is listed with a new thought, a new idea. These paragraphs are a collection of wisdom from the books that I have written over these many years of work and joy and travel with these higher beings of light from the Himalayas, to South America, to Europe, to Australia, and Asia. I want to share with you the beauty of this journey in short meditations, thoughts, paragraphs that I think will give you or help you find inspiration within your days. May you journey with soft winds at your back.

INTRODUCTION

In spirit and love

JANUARY

PLANT YOUR SEEDS

Take responsibility for your world. Plant your seeds for new beginnings with great care. When you plant a seed, you are planting and cultivating energy, the energy of the life force that will send that seed on its journey toward the light so that it can blossom and become a manifested reality.

Lynn Andrews
Coming Full Circle

TRUE ESSENCE

An act of power is an expression in the world of your true essence. If you don't have an act of power, you can never really see who you are.

Lynn Andrews
Love and Power

PERCEIVE THE LIGHT

Sometimes the light can be too bright, too painful to look at. So if you can't yet adjust to the light of something, you perceive it in another way. You open your body-mind and perceive light like Ruby does. She absorbs light and shadow through her intent and has learned to see that way with her blind eyes. That's why no one is more aware than Ruby. There is nothing that she cannot see—even in total darkness. For her, there is always light, and it can no longer be taken from her.

Agnes Whistling Elk
Dark Sister

SPIRIT OF A WARRIORESS

You are a born fighter. Many people do not under-stand the spirit of a warrioress. The whole world will seem to be against you, but you will never surrender. You will shift and move down alternate trails and become invisible in the wilderness, but you will fight to the death to protect your destiny.

Ginevee
Crystal Woman

TRUTH

Are you living your truth? Your being is like a spirit
lodge. Within this sacred place is your realization
and the divine light of your creation. Live in your
spirit lodge surrounded by peace and joy.

Lynn Andrews
The Power Deck

SPEAK TO SPIRIT—LISTEN TO POWER

An eagle soars above and sees all the vast complexities and interrelationships. When an eagle feather falls from a medicine eagle to the earth, it is full of that knowledge. If you're smart, you will talk to that eagle feather and ask the spirit of it to guide you. All eagle feathers have that power. You have to pick it up and talk to it. Then you have to know how to listen to the answer.

Agnes Whistling Elk
Medicine Woman

SING YOUR SONG

In the Tree of Dreams there is a song. Like any
other living thing, it has a song to be sung. To lose
your song is to lose your soul. The song in the trees
is something to be listened for very, very carefully.
It teaches you that life is never-ending.

Grandmother
Tree of Dreams

SACRED DREAMING

"Dreaming spans the worlds. Lay your head in the west each night and lead your life among simple things. In the heart below the feathered bonnet of illumination, return to your true self, where there are no separations." Twin Dreamers raised her arm and pointed upward. "Before you is the universe. Remember that all things are sacred."

Twin Dreamers and Lynn Andrews
Star Woman

NOTHING IS AS IT SEEMS

"I cannot imagine my life without you, Agnes."

"But you see, it is not as it appears," Agnes said. She tapped the top of the table with her knuckles. "Nothing is as it seems. You must remember this and never forget it. When you are no longer an apprentice, then you will be a true teacher. Then your apprenticeship is to someone different. It is to the Great Spirit. It is to the great deities that live on the other side. It is only then that you will learn what true apprenticeship really means."

Agnes Whistling Elk and Lynn Andrews
Shakkai, Woman of the Sacred Garden

STAR PODS

In a sense we are all star pods on this earth with a destiny to become enlightened, to create mirrors in our lifetime through the process of movement and life force, mirrors that enhance our fulfillment and the evolvement of our spirit. We have an ancient longing to return home, home to the source of all that is.

Lynn Andrews
Woman at the Edge of Two Worlds Workbook

IN BEAUTY IS TRUTH

In beauty is truth. In this simple statement is
found all the power that you will ever need in
life. Find what is beautiful for you and you will
find your truth. Find your truth and you
will find your power.

Lynn Andrews
Coming Full Circle

TAKING THE BAIT

The most important thing about any trap is the bait. When you use water for bait, remember that it will be thirst that pulls the game. If you know the right bait, you can trap any being you want, but only if you know how to make the right trap as well. Learn the true character of an animal or a thing before you hunt it.

Agnes Whistling Elk
Medicine Woman

PASSION

Embrace the life of a wanderer, finding oceans
of joy in the unknown path to the next horizon.
Find a different kind of security—one that is deep
within your heart, in a place of peace and well-
being; it is the treasure of your hero's journey.

Lynn Andrews
Sacred Vision Oracle Cards

TRUST YOUR SEEING

Picking mushrooms is hard. You have to be like a mushroom yourself to find them under the pine needles in the forest. Just like what you see about yourself now—the truth, like the mushrooms. It was there all the time. You just didn't see it.

Ruby Plenty Chiefs
Tree of Dreams

LOOK INTO THE SHADOWS

Beauty always has another side. If you look at something carefully, as a Medicine Woman, you will always be able to see the dark side too. One cannot exist without the other and yet, people choose never to look into the shadows.
They fear the devil.

Butterfly Woman
Jaguar Woman

YOUR SEASONS OF EXISTENCE

You are a Tree of Dreams and your act of power lives within the very fibers and cells and being-ness of this tree that you are. Your act of power has a cycle that is similar to a great tree. Your act of power moves through the seasons of existence, the budding, the blooming, the falling of your leaves or your needles, the shedding and sharing of your manifestations with the world, and then you rest within the wintering of your dreams and realization.

Lynn Andrews
Writing Spirit

SHADOW SHIELD

If you repress your natural instincts, whatever they may be, they create a shadow self. It's part of your shadow shield, the darkness. How that instinctual nature is suppressed and what you have allowed yourself to do in ceremony to heal it depend on many things, such as on your history, your spirit history.

Zoila
Dark Sister

BE HERE NOW

Nothing is ever enough if you don't accept yourself right this moment as complete. If you don't, there will always be a sense of longing, and you will die with that longing even if you are a famous writer, or invincible as a healer.

Agnes Whistling Elk
Star Woman

DEFINE YOUR OWN SACRED LIFE

Symbolically speaking, you cannot always take
a costume or a tradition that is created by someone else for their ceremonies and expect to put
that costume or ritual on and experience the same
sacredness that they had. That's because it's not
your costume. You need to design your own.

Agnes Whistling Elk
Tree of Dreams

PRAY

Oh Great Spirit,
The sacred blanket of life
Keeps me warm when I am cold.
In these days of transition,
I take the sacred blankets
That you have given us,
And I remember how
You taught us to pray.

Lynn Andrews
Walk in Spirit: Prayers for the Seasons of Life

THE SPIRAL

Agnes pushed her finger in the middle of the dust spiral. "When you are born, you come from the void. You come from the mystery. You are born out of formlessness from the center of the spiral."

Agnes Whistling Elk and Lynn Andrews
Star Woman

STAY BALANCED

Power comes from a sense of focus, well-being, and health, all of which emanate from maintaining a balanced point of view in the world. Power is the energy that flows through all things. Individuals earn access to it by keeping themselves healthy and strong physically, emotionally, and spiritually. We become healthy when we heal the dis-ease in our spirits. The contentment of the soul becomes reflected in our bodies as a glowing state of health and an absence of illness.

Lynn Andrews
Love and Power

INSECURITY

You create your own insecurity. Insecurity is a great addiction. Like any other addiction it robs you of your strength. You use it like a prop, the way many of our brothers and sisters use alcohol or anything else. But that prop can kill you. You see it as a defense against the unknowable. When we get too close to something we don't understand, we reach for our props, our addictions. With those addictions we destroy our Seeing, and the unknowable seems much further away. What is really further away is the realization of your original nature, that part of you that is the All Mother.

Ginevee
Crystal Woman

BE DANGEROUS

You can only be dangerous when you accept your
death. Then you become dangerous in spite of
anything. You must learn to see the awake ones.
A dangerous woman can do anything because
she will do anything. A powerful woman will do
the unthinkable because the unthinkable belongs
to her. Everything belongs to her, and anything
is possible. She can track her vision and kill it
by making it come true.

Agnes Whistling Elk
Medicine Woman

WE ARE THE LIGHT

The tree is a way into life. There are many trees,
Lynn, and many myths and legends concerning
them. Right now I would like to tell you another
of these myths. Always look for the truth beyond
the words. The Sisterhood of the Shields tells us of
the first tree, also called Sky Tree of Man, or simply
butterfly tree. This is the tree of all the ancestors;
it is where first man and first woman came from.
Tree Mother suckled them.

The sisters say that upon the branches of this tree are billions and billions of leaves. Written upon these leaves is the destiny of each new person. So when a person is born, a leaf falls from the butterfly tree. The spirit light descends from one of these leaves and surrounds the egg at conception.

It is a person's destiny to realize that we are one with the sacred tree. We are not just a leaf. We are the light. And we are the light of the butterfly tree.

Agnes Whistling Elk and Lynn Andrews
Jaguar Woman

OPEN YOURSELF

Welcome passion and creativity into your hut and make them your partners, and be amazed as you awaken the abilities and the brilliance that already reside within you.

Lynn Andrews
Coming Full Circle

CIRCUMSTANCE

I felt the west wind pushing against my back as though it were supporting my efforts and had come to encourage me. I contemplated the magnificence of this life. I saw more clearly than I ever had that we are all exactly in the position in life that we choose to be in, no more or less. We are not victims of circumstance. We have formed our own circumstance for many complex reasons, which often remain unnamed out of our own ignorance or our inability to learn and face the truth.

Lynn Andrews
Star Woman

HONOR THE DARK SIDE

When women understand their Ultima Madre,
or final mother, they can build altars and fetishes
of these powers. When they feel the influence of
Crazy Woman or the Death Mother, in the form
of depression or gloom, they can light candles and
burn copal and honor her great power, the dark
side. You see, her intent only defines your goodness
and beauty. By honoring the dark side, you destroy
her power over you. Then she can't take you.

Zoila
Jaguar Woman

FIND YOUR CIRCLE OF LIFE

"I see a dream for your people, black wolf," she said, her eyes glittering, not unlike the timber wolves that I have seen. "The dream that I see for your people is to find a circle of life that honors your elders, something that your people have forgotten. I know that you spend a great deal of time in life trying to encourage the growth of this concept with our sister, Face in the Water. I'm going to place this dream in the center of this circle, and we will make it so. I make this bid for power."

Twin Dreamers and Lynn Andrews
Tree of Dreams

WHO ARE YOU?

My teacher Agnes Whistling Elk once asked me, "And what have you learned, my daughter, from all the work that we have done together?"

I was very excited and said, "Well, I have learned to be a healer. I have learned to do acts of power in the world, and I am an author."

"No, my daughter," she admonished, "you are a woman living her truth who happens to write, who happens to heal and work with people."

Agnes Whistling Elk and Lynn Andrews
Love and Power

JACKRABBITS

"Your moods make rabbits today," Agnes, who sat next to me, whispered in my ear.

"What do you mean?" She had startled me.

"You think little thoughts and they multiply like jackrabbits."

Agnes Whistling Elk and Lynn Andrews
Crystal Woman

FEBRUARY

IMAGINATION

Know that what you imagine is real. In this pragmatic life, we forget the importance of imagination. Imagination and visualization can be at the root of your successful ceremony called life.

Lynn Andrews
The Power Deck

WHAT IS YOUR POLLEN?

Nature, when you experience the majesty and the
beauty in her, has the ability to transform you.
I remember the first time I met Zoila. As we were
speaking in her garden, an exquisite iridescent
green hummingbird flew between us and explored
a fuchsia bush. Zoila nodded toward it and told
me, "Watch how the hummingbird uses power."
The hummingbird hovered in front of the flower,
sensing whether its pollen was right. Pollen
is power to this bird, a tiny bird that is, itself,
so powerful that some migrate a few thousand
miles each spring and fall.

Lynn Andrews
Coming Full Circle

WRITE YOUR OWN STORY

"But we do live forever," Ruby said, rejoining the conversation and sitting next to me. I noticed she had tied deer rattles around her ankles. They made a beautiful sound like rushing water. "You're afraid of death, Lynn," said Ruby. "Strangely enough, in your relationship with Red Dog, you're finding the end of that trail. Our lives are inspired by the Great Spirit. You're beginning to see beyond a shadow of a doubt that the more light you have, the more life. Death serves to bring things sharply into focus. You have moved in and out of this focus all of your life. It has charted your fate. Now you are taking the feathered quill in your own hand and beginning to write your own story."

Ruby Plenty Chiefs and Lynn Andrews
Tree of Dreams

FEBRUARY 4

EXPAND YOUR HEART

Sit beneath this waterfall and allow the power and flow of this water to enter you. Allow your thoughts to fall away and your heart to expand, and experience your own truth. Let your mind and body be set free. Let your being be supple and empty. Let your mind flow downriver with the water. Allow yourself to be in touch in the most loving way with the real "living midnight" that lives inside you. It is the arousal of your positive energies. You do not need me. You do not need anyone. Because of that, you are ready for love.

Shakkai
Shakkai, Woman of the Sacred Garden

FACE THE CORRECT WIND ROAD

See the nature of the winds that approach you.
Some winds are friendly and will play with
you. There are hot and cold winds. There are
crazy winds that can seize your mind. There are
trickster winds that you can follow at your
own peril. There are mother and father winds.
There are medicine winds and virtuous
winds. There are winds low to the ground,
earth huggers, and those high above your head.
To know the wind, you study the winged ones.
They know the winds better than anybody.

Ruby Plenty Chiefs
Star Woman

BOOMERANG EFFECT

"Some energy you can thrust out into the
sacred rounds of life and it will return to
you like a boomerang."

"What kind of energy is that, Agnes?"

"The energy of creativity. Energy always returns
to its source when it is born of creativity."

Agnes Whistling Elk and Lynn Andrews
Crystal Woman

THE GREAT DANCE OF LIFE

Shamanism is a powerful and beautiful worldview, born of the interconnectedness of all living things in the universe, both seen and unseen. What an exquisite way to know sacredness, that we are all part of the great One and that the Oneness of life flows through all living things, plant and animal alike, the winds, the seas, the rains, the world of spirit and the world of the physical, even other universes, connecting all that is in the great dance we humans call life.

Lynn Andrews
Coming Full Circle

THE VOICE OF WISDOM IS WITHIN

It is my belief that the Great Spirit is in all things,
and all things are within the Great Spirit.
We are all part of the great oneness of life.

Lynn Andrews
Sacred Vision Oracle Cards

PULL DOWN THE CLOUDS

"You must imitate the exact event you desire,"
Agnes said as she knelt down and touched the
rain-soaked earth from the night before. "Like this
ground that has drunk its fill, you must saturate
your being with whatever it is you are looking for.
Follow your ideas about death, life, and immor-
tality. Understand that you are pulling down the
clouds." Agnes pointed to the sky. "You are calling
for rain in your heart so that your spirit can grow."

Agnes Whistling Elk and Lynn Andrews
Tree of Dreams

THERE IS ONLY LIFE

We can never explain the mysteries of the Great
Spirit. Why does power work in the way it does?
This is not for me to explain or even to bother
myself with. All I'm concerned about is what is.
There is no "normal life" or explaining the
"challenge of life." There is only life.

Agnes Whistling Elk
Dark Sister

ALLOW CHANGE

Your world needs the balance between the strong male shield and the strong female shield. You have to learn how to balance these energies in yourselves and in your world without dropping one or the other. When you drop one or the other shield, you lose the vision, the insight, the power that shield gives you. You have to learn what the male shield is all about and what the female shield is all about. The male shield teaches you to move out into the world in an organized and forceful way so that you can be effective in your endeavors. The female shield takes you into your intuition, teaching you to be receptive to the energy that is going on around you so that you will understand it and know how to move through it successfully, receptive to new ideas.

Twin Dreamers
Coming Full Circle

FEAR: THE GREAT MOTIVATOR

Fear is a great motivator. None of us like to be in
fear, but there are times when it makes us move.
It makes us move when we're stuck.

Lynn Andrews
Woman at the Edge of Two Worlds

BE PHENOMENAL

Whether it's being a phenomenal cook, somebody
who can wash a dish better than anybody else, or
something else. Be a star in your own world, whatever that is, but make the effort. Find the intent
and the courage to do it.

Lynn Andrews
Love and Power

JUST DO IT

Agnes, Ruby, Zoila, and Twin Dreamers had one thing in common: They had all looked at the horizon line of their respective lives and had seen that it appeared flat. Each in her own way had made a choice, irrespective of what they believed to be right and true. Each recognized the fact that if she saw a destiny in her own path, the only way to fulfill that destiny was to simply do it. As Ruby had so often said to me, "You either do it or you don't. Don't mealymouth around about why nobody understands your purpose in life. You're just holding up the wrong pictures. Change the pictures if you have to."

Ruby Plenty Chiefs and Lynn Andrews
Star Woman

BELIEVE IN MAGIC

There is magic in this world if you want
the world to be magical. If you want life
to be special, it will be.

Lynn Andrews
Tree of Dreams

SEE THE TRUTH

When you see only darkness, you can perceive
almost nothing that is happening around you—
it's as if you are blind, even with your eyes open.
It's very simple. The light, sunlight or wisdom, illu-
minates what is there. Simple and true—ignorance
is born from not seeing what is there in front of
you. When you live in the darkness of your soul,
you cannot see the truth, a chair, an idea, or whatever is in existence for your benefit.

Agnes Whistling Elk
Dark Sister

SEED POD

We can become anything we want to be. As a seed pod, there is a destiny that was written by the gods long before you were formed. So remember that destiny of beauty and perfection as you lay dormant now through the long winter. Imagine yourself as having been planted somewhere in the earth. Feel the nurturing energy of Mother Earth holding you.

Lynn Andrews
Woman at the Edge of Two Worlds Workbook

HONOR YOUR FLAWS

Life is a wonder and is absurd because it exists without explanation. Perfection requires explanation, does it not? Living life is about honoring your vulnerabilities. Whether you know it or not, you are entering a new world through your flaws as well as your talents, and this new world exists in a more vibrant state of mind.

Lynn Andrews
Writing Spirit

REBIRTH

"I remember what Shakkai was telling me. She was saying that when you die, it is simply a passage into the next dimension where you will not have only three dimensions, but four—four different aspects of perception. Is that true?"

Ruby nodded and Agnes agreed. "Yes, it is true, but not in the way you think."

"What do you mean?" I asked.

"There are lifetimes of being reborn into this physical world, and once you've learned what you need to learn in physical relativity, then you move to the next dimension. Sometimes it takes a long, long time to get to that so-called fourth dimension in the sense of your rebirth patterns. You can only deal with the reality of the moment."

I suddenly realized that if you don't solve a problem of hate or love or a struggle in one lifetime, it moves on to the next dimension. It moves on to the next life.

Agnes Whistling Elk, Ruby Plenty Chiefs, and Lynn Andrews
Shakkai, Woman of the Sacred Garden

YOUR SONG

"You have taught me the joys of elderhood. I want others to be inspired by that vision. I want to tell these stories well. I want to write a book, Grandmother, that has chapters in it that represent leaves falling from the Tree of Dreams."

"You have your song," she said. "You learned about the ways of power early in your work with us. As long as you have your song, you can never lose your direction or your vision."

Face in the Water and Lynn Andrews
Tree of Dreams

SMOKE IS PRAYER

Quite suddenly the moon went behind more clouds, and we were plunged into a thick, pungent darkness. The fire crackled and glowed. Two red coals shone like the eyes of a dragon, and then even they dimmed. For several minutes nothing could be seen. The smoke had a sweet, unfamiliar odor. I coughed a couple of times.

"In your mind, Lynn, go to the smoke," Agnes said. "Become the smoke. Smoke is prayer. Your spirit will strengthen there. Dream."

Agnes Whistling Elk and Lynn Andrews
Star Woman

YOUR LONG JOURNEY

You are about to go on a long journey. It is a
journey of life and death. You will learn to heal the
evil forces of darkness. You are a warrioress in the
fight against ignorance. The sorcerers in life are
created within each of us.

Ginevee
Crystal Woman

FIRST STEPS

Knowledge is the first step toward wisdom, which is found in the balance between universal knowledge and the sanctuary of knowledge that is learned through our harmony and our struggles on Mother Earth. In wisdom, there is no fear. So if something impacts you so greatly as to ignite your fear or your anger, then make it important enough to learn about. Find out about it from as many different perspectives as you can.

Lynn Andrews
Coming Full Circle

YOU ARE MADE OF ENERGY

Energy is life. Everything is made of energy, including you. Energy is power. If you don't truly understand that you are made of energy, that you are a moving life force that needs direction and intent, then you cannot express who you are in society in a meaningful way. To achieve balance and harmony in your life, you need an understanding of energy. Energy is the whirling protons, electrons, and neutrons that produce friction and heat. But what creates the force, the life spirit? God.

Lynn Andrews
Love and Power

WISE BLOOD

Don't give away your power—remember who you are. When your heart beats, it is the pulsation of the Great Goddess Mother's heart. You are the one, and you are one with all that lives. When you breathe, it is the Great Spirit who breathes. When you grieve, it is the Goddess Spirit that grieves. When you bleed, it is Mother Earth who bleeds, and when you hold your power and your blood, it is the Goddess Spirit of wise blood becoming whole within you.

Woman at the Edge of Two Worlds
Woman at the Edge of Two Worlds

I CLAIM MY WONDER

"I like to speak of the essence of things. We get lost in our physical lives. Your people, your dear wonderful people, are so filled with stress and consternation. With all your institutions of higher learning, your people still don't know what they are doing on the most simple, basic foundations of life. You have it all in your hands, like treasures of gold, but you don't see it. Your insistence on control and war is beyond my imagination and my ability to handle the sadness that it causes me."

Twin Dreamers and Lynn Andrews
Coming Full Circle

BLISS

At the core of all creation myths is movement, and deeper into the process of movement is the silent darkness of bliss and nothingness from which all comes and to which all returns. We are made from stars and to the stars we must return one day.

Lynn Andrews
Woman at the Edge of Two Worlds Workbook

WALK ALL THE TRAILS

Out of loss is created great mysteries of beauty and ability. When our people lost everything, we created another world to go to, and we experience the nagual worlds of beauty and dreaming. We are never born and we never die, and for the spirit there is great comfort in this knowledge. Share it with those who want to know.

Jaguar Woman
Dark Sister

MARCH

SISTER STARS

"Don't you know I am looking into your eyes? You think no one is there, but I am here, looking, waiting for you to see me. See me, black wolf, in all of your beauty and your power. You must not give yourself away like this. In the emptiness of space, feel your sister stars around you. They are blessing you and keeping you from harm."

Agnes Whistling Elk and Lynn Andrews
Tree of Dreams

HOW YOU LIVE MATTERS

Then I saw Agnes's face in my mind's eye, smiling at me, as she had, not long ago, as we sat on a log in the horse pasture near her cabin. "If you are a sacred being, it does not matter what you do or where you live. All that matters is how you live, because sacredness is part of balance. If you can live, Lynn, in Los Angeles and maintain your balance and the purity of your spirit, you can live anywhere. It is very much easier to live in a protected monastery as a monk in the Himalayas and remain spiritually balanced. It is very difficult to have one foot in the physical manifestation of a chaotic city and to keep the other foot firmly implanted in the land of healthy spirit. It is one of the reasons I sent you home. I sent you there because it is the people of the cities who need to be healed. It is the people of the cities who lose their souls first."

Agnes Whistling Elk and Lynn Andrews
Woman at the Edge of Two Worlds

UNDERSTAND THE DARKNESS

If we do not honor the dark side, then we will be ruled by the dark side. Always remember that if you become what you are trying to defeat, then what you are trying to defeat wins. When something negative affects you powerfully, you must look at it and understand it, and then turn your face away and let the light be your guide. To understand the darkness does not mean you become it. It means you examine it carefully, learning what it is made of, understanding its power and its limitations. Only then can you really do something to change it.

Lynn Andrews
Coming Full Circle

YOUR TRUTH

Don't ever let anyone else tell you who or what
you should think or be in life. Don't let other
people interpret life for you. Their truth may be
very different from yours, and then where
will you be?

Lynn Andrews
Sacred Vision Oracle Cards

YOU ARE HOME

Sometimes you don't realize that you're home.
You don't realize what you have until you lose it.
It's one of the greatest lessons of any lifetime
on the path of spirit.

Agnes Whistling Elk
Dark Sister

DEFINE YOUR REALITY

How you express your power helps define your reality. Your use of that power—your intellect, vision, integrity, and intent—defines your relationship with people and the world around you. When you assume power in a conscious way, always balance it with love, if not for a person, then for animals, art, or nature, so that your life becomes more successful, and more harmonious in every respect.

Lynn Andrews
Love and Power

LESSONS OF POWER

Shamanism is about the end of duality. It is about oneness with all of the energies that surround you. If you do not understand the oneness of energy, you do not understand the laws of power. The first lesson of power is that we are all alone. And then there is a giant abyss between this statement and the last lesson of power, which is that we are all one. The last lesson of power is the oneness of us all, the respect and the honor given to different ideologies and thought, not war between those ideologies but honor.

Lynn Andrews
Writing Spirit

LESSONS OF SUFFERING

"You learned to study your own suffering so
that the suffering of others could be understood.
Teach your apprentices not to distract themselves
from their pain. Lead them into the center
of pain, to confront it."

Ginevee nodded toward Booru, who was still
holding up the night-blooming herb. "Suffering
is like the seed of that herb when planted in the
earth. That seed remembers itself and endures in
the darkness so that it can grow up into the sunlight one day as an entirely transformed flower.
When you understand suffering and the forces
of darkness you can end suffering and bring
light to the people."

Ginevee and Lynn Andrews
Crystal Woman

OUR INNER ORACLE

We have within ourselves that teacher, that healer
we seek. We each have an inner oracle who knows
what is wrong, how it got there, and what to do
about it. Self-healing is about getting in touch with
that inner ability to know the truth and using it to
transform our issues and wounds into beauty
and strength as we heal.

Lynn Andrews
Inner Oracle, Online Course

NEVER GIVE AWAY YOUR POWER

Jaguar Woman had placed her shield on top of Sin Corazón's shield with no respect for what Sin Corazón's shield was, the beauty of it, the fragility of it, the perfection of it. She saw Jaguar Woman destroying the perfection of it with her own shield. Then Jaguar Woman stepped onto the shields, grinding them even farther into the dirt, and she said, "Never forget. This is what most people do to each other. They place their shields on top of your own and say that they are theirs. They destroy your vision and ask you to live their own. This is the way of most marriages, of most relationships. Be careful in your life and never give away the power of your shield to someone else."

continued on next page

continued from previous page

Then she had gone over and taken her shield off Sin Corazón's and placed it next to Sin Corazón's.

"This is as it should be. Two shields flying through the universe together in perfect harmony and perfect balance."

Jaguar Woman, Sin Corazón, and Lynn Andrews
Dark Sister

WITNESS YOUR TRUTH

"Lama Shingdo has decided to dismember the corpse and feed it to the vultures. It is good. Bahni has lived a good life," Ani said.

I stopped in my tracks.

"Ani, I can't do this. I can't watch such a thing. I cannot bear the reality of this kind of funeral." I sat down on the path and clutched my shawl around me and put it over the back of my head, sobbing.

continued on next page

MARCH 11

continued from previous page

"Reality does not disappear because of death. Life is eternal. In reality there is no death. What you will be watching is the dismemberment of maya, of the illusion, of the dream that we call life. What you fear is not the spectacle, but the truth that you are witnessing. It is your own truth, not Bahni's. She has already moved into luminosity. She has journeyed into what is real. You know you've lost the trail. You know in your heart"—Ani poked my chest—"what dies is only the unreal. Death proves that."

Ani and Lynn Andrews
Windhorse Woman

YOUR ALLY WIND

"Look at it this way, Lynn," Agnes said, sensing my fear and running her hand down my arm to calm me. "The wind is a singer, the greatest singer that ever was. There are a million tunes, symphonies. But your ears are little. I don't mean in size. I mean little in hearing ability. If you had ears for the wind and would listen, you would never be without a song. The wind climbers, the fliers, hear this music and are called to it. The wind can be an ally wind."

Agnes Whistling Elk and Lynn Andrews
Star Woman

ACCESS THE INNER VOICE

Passivity can be an integral aspect of great power, as when we sit in total stillness and allow the bedlam of life to go on around us while we focus on connecting with our inner voice of truth. It takes enormous personal strength to be able to do this. Passivity allows us to access the inner voice that tells us what is right and what is not right in any given situation, as opposed to reacting out of fear, greed, or judgment.

Lynn Andrews
Coming Full Circle

WISDOM KEEPER

Love for other human beings is the reason we do our work at all. We care about the balance of this magnificent earth we live on. We care about preserving her magic and her power. There are few people in the world that can do what we can. There are few who can commit this knowledge to memory and pass it on to our apprentices and our daughters and sons. Because of that, we have to put knowledge first. We are the keepers of the wisdom of Wyrrd, and that is a great and extraordinary responsibility. You know that you have been born to this destiny. There are certain people in every time who feel this destiny and are drawn to the truth.

Alice and Catherine
The Woman of Wyrrd

ESSENCE

We come onto this earthwalk like a giant piece
of smashed mirror, every one of us reflecting the
light of our god. The experience of life is a process
of piecing together these scrambled fragments
into one great mandala, reflecting the one
source of all being.

Lynn Andrews
The Power Deck

SMALL DEATHS

It takes great strength to have the freedom to die with grace and allow the last of life to slip away gracefully. We all are faced with our own mortality. You don't need to have constant excitement in your life to feel alive. But sometimes the small deaths—grief, loss, hard decisions—teach you how to live.

Lynn Andrews
Tree of Dreams

WHY ARE YOU AFRAID?

"Why are we so afraid of realizing ourselves?" July asked. She slowed the truck to let five white-faced Hereford cows mosey across the road.

"Because we're like those cows," Agnes answered. "It's easier just to follow along in the herd, chewing our cuds and psychically asleep. We've come here to enter the sacred rounds, to be enlightened. You're not here to be a mother, a daughter, a writer. You're here to learn. I've told you this before, Lynn and July. We're the most afraid of the one thing we've come here to do. And that is to grow and become self-realized."

**Agnes Whistling Elk, July,
and Lynn Andrews**
Star Woman

YOUR PLACE OF POWER

No matter what religion, no matter what nationality, the greatest teachings always move you into a place of power within yourself. You do not place power outside yourself. Truth is a reflection of the Great Spirit, always living within your own heart.

Lynn Andrews
Woman at the Edge of Two Worlds

MEDICINE POWER

Medicine power is the power to bring harmony and balance into your life and into the life of others. When you begin to balance yourself in a medicine way, you begin to see magical glimpses because you are telling the beings of the earth that you believe in beauty. You are becoming beauty. To learn medicine is to spin or to weave the concept of life into tangible forms, to lift beyond your ordinary vision and see the forces that give us life. This is why I am teaching you to understand things with all of your being, with all of your senses.

Agnes Whistling Elk
Inner Oracle, Online Course

NEW BEGINNINGS

Spring is the time of new beginnings, when the
trees bud and rains prepare the soil for new growth.
For millenniums, farmers have planted their seeds
with great care during the springtime so that they
will weather the storms of the season that bring
much needed moisture and fertilization.
Look at the seeds you are going to sow
and make critical decisions.

Lynn Andrews
Coming Full Circle

THE GIFT OF LIFE

You are flowering now. You are in your prime.
Celebrate. Celebrate the magnificence of your
body. Dance in celebration for the mystery
and the gift of life.

Lynn Andrews
Woman at the Edge of Two Worlds Workbook

TWISTED HAIR

"Jaguar Woman is one of the greatest Twisted Hairs among us. She is a consummate Storyteller," Agnes said.

"What makes her such a great Storyteller?" I asked.

"Because she knows how to take herself out of the story," Ruby answered for Agnes. "She knows how to completely remove herself, as if she were a fly on the wall with no self-importance. If she happens to be in the story, she speaks of herself as if she is simply part of the tale. She weaves a sacred dream. She takes words like threads, magnificently luminous and colored with the light of creation, and weaves them together with magic and power into a tapestry so that the story lives for you. She is like no other Storyteller I have been graced to hear. There is much for you to learn in these stories. Be aware. Do not miss anything."

Agnes Whistling Elk, Ruby Plenty Chiefs, and Lynn Andrews
Dark Sister

THE GODDESS OF CHANGE

"We have to take our power as women. That doesn't mean become less female. It means to take our place as the goddess, as Xochiquetzal. She is the goddess of change," Zoila said. "She is the mother of us all. She is like your White Buffalo Woman. We women must be that in whatever aspect. Then we can teach our men how to live. Otherwise all is lost."

**Zoila, Ruby Plenty Chiefs,
and Lynn Andrews**
Star Woman

BECOME TRULY ENLIGHTENED

Enlightenment is the expulsion of darkness. We use faith as a burning candle, yet all light casts shadows. It is into these gray and black areas that we must traverse to truly become enlightened.

Lynn Andrews
Sacred Vision Oracle Cards

FIND THE JOY

We cannot change people; people have to change themselves. That takes a special awareness and a perception of beauty and joy in life around us. If you can't find the joy in a magnificent sunset, or an eagle in flight, or a baby horse with big innocent eyes, if you can't see the beauty, nobody can force you. Something in you has to change in order for you to perceive the aesthetics and take them into your soul and illuminate yourself with the joy of the creation of life.

Lynn Andrews
Love and Power

YOUR TRUE IDENTITY

"Watch carefully, Lynn," Agnes whispered in my ear. "You are seeing all that you are, your visible and invisible identities." For a moment, I thought I would lose my self-control. Then Agnes whispered again, "But it's not enough to experience your true identity. If you think you are powerless, you cannot live. You will be locked in endless grappling and violence within the circle of self. Overcome your hesitancy and become strong. Fend off your doubts. Dream your sacred dream."

Agnes Whistling Elk and Lynn Andrews
Star Woman

CLEAR IN SPIRIT

To stay in form, you must have difficulties. If you are clear in your spirit, if you are truly weightless in your being, then you will leave your form and you will move on to another dimension.

Shakkai
Shakkai, Woman of the Sacred Garden

TAKE A RISK

Nobody owns the truth. Why are we so quick
to give our truth away when someone disagrees
with us or doesn't give us the encouragement that
we expected? If you believe in your dreams, isn't
it worth taking the risk of bringing them to life?
Your life is worth the risk. Living your truth is your
heritage. It is your birthright, a right that is not
available to all people across the world.

Lynn Andrews
Love and Power

SUMMON THE CLOUDS

"You know, Lynn, you are ready," Agnes said.

"Ready for what?" I asked.

"For a new mountain to climb," she said with a wave of her hand. "You are preparing for something that you have never really taken on."

"What is that?" I asked quietly. A slow apprehension was beginning to build in my heart.

"You are approaching the moon of rain. It rains a great deal, but then the rain ceases to fall and the desert returns and the cactuses bloom, displaying their spring beauty," Agnes said. "Sometimes the clouds don't come and the rain is late and the corn and the grass do not grow. Then your thirst will transform your spirit."

"And you will drink the nectar of the thunder beings," Ruby stated very clearly.

"There are many threads to be woven together," Agnes added.

I thought about their words and how they expressed the simplest nature of life: rain, corn, earth. "Where do I fit in?" I finally asked.

"You summon the clouds," Agnes said. "You must allow the many things that will happen to you. You must accept them completely; just as the earth and the cactus fill up with rain. You take your spirit back. Not only for yourself, but for us."

Agnes Whistling Elk, Ruby Plenty Chiefs, and Lynn Andrews
Tree of Dreams

MARCH 30

KINDRED SPIRITS

People are known by the stories they tell. Your stories are constructs of the people you have met along your journey. Ultimately, the grandest and most beautiful is the story of meeting and sharing the journey with a kindred spirit—a true friend.

Lynn Andrews
Sacred Vision Oracle Cards

REALITY CHECK

Sometimes a truth has to hurt a bit
to be remembered.

Agnes Whistling Elk
Dark Sister

APRIL

BE MINDFUL

Build your life's foundation on perfected moments of kindness and joy, and be mindful of the words that you use. Words present a powerful duality, containing the energy to create and to destroy. How will you use yours?

Lynn Andrews
Sacred Vision Oracle Cards

MAKING PEACE

"Our people speak of making peace," Shakkai said with a serious tone to her voice, searching carefully for the words to impart this knowledge to me. "It is comfortable and easy for us to talk about making peace, making love, giving love, giving action out into the world. That is where the mind is comfortable, and the ego is very comfortable with that idea, because in fact ego is mind. It is a much more difficult thing to put oneself into a humble stance and receive that love, receive peace into one's own heart and being."

Shakkai and Lynn Andrews
Shakkai, Woman of the Sacred Garden

ZEN

When you think of doing your heart's desire, when you think about manifesting intent into the world, to me that is like Zen painting. If I look at a Zen painting, I feel a kind of joy. I feel uplifted. I feel my energy rise. I don't know how anyone could feel otherwise. Zen painting makes you want to play music or sing or tell everybody about what you are manifesting.

Lynn Andrews
Writing Spirit

CHANGE IS LAW

I want you to see that if you believe that something is a square when actually it's a circle, then you will probably believe that for all your life. Life is full of change. It is the law. It has always been that way.

Agnes Whistling Elk
Tree of Dreams

EBB AND FLOW

There is a meadow that I go to in Montana that is at the foot of the mountains, and I always know that the water will be running there. Life flows in the same way. There is an ebbing and a flowing, like the tides at the ocean shore, of life and life force. The force of life flows through us all throughout existence. We are really not separate. We are all one, just like single drops in the flowing water coming down from the mountains. Each drop becomes part of the greater whole. The river and the flow will go on forever. The water will eventually reach the sea. Then it will evaporate into the clouds, and again there will be rain and snow and the whole process will be started all over again.

Lynn Andrews
Woman at the Edge of Two Worlds

APRIL 6

HUNTING

I wanted to know more about hunting, but Agnes
was finished. "I have to give you power to be effective," she said, "not ideas you don't know from your
own inner voice, not borrowed knowledge.
You want to have ability, don't you?
You can't talk an animal to death."

Agnes Whistling Elk and Lynn Andrews
Medicine Woman

HUMOR

We need our sense of humor to remember that it
is dangerous to be caught in the dream, to lose the
understanding that the reality of life as we know
it is only an illusion.

Lynn Andrews
The Power Deck

PEELING AWAY THE LAYERS

Searching for wisdom and self-empowerment is a necessary part of life. Moving forward and peeling away the levels of negative conditioning through communication can bring each individual to mastery. Together, we have realized that this is not a selfish process, but an essential one, a necessary part of the power of love. The mastery of our lives needs to be understood fully.

Lynn Andrews
Love and Power

HISTORY KEEPERS

Crystals, just like the ones in our computers, hold memory. They can help you recall your life history and the healing you have experienced over your many lifetimes. Crystals and stones are the keepers of history. They can help you remember what you came here to do and the powers and gifts you brought with you into this lifetime. Too often we forget ourselves, and crystals awaken us to our magnificence.

Lynn Andrews
Return to Wholeness, Online Course

CIRCLE OF HARMONY

Great Spirit, whose voice we hear
In the winds and the trees,
Mother Earth, whose breath gives us life:
Help us to walk in beauty and strength,
And to learn the lessons that are hidden
In the stones and the trees
And the waters of the sea.
Give us the strength to fight
Our greatest enemy—ignorance.

Lynn Andrews
Walk in Spirit

SPIT

We fished for more than an hour. Agnes and July
were thoroughly frustrated. None of us had caught
anything except Ruby, who got several browns and
rainbows. "All right, Ruby," Agnes said frowning.
"What's your secret? What are we doing wrong?"

"Wrong? Why, nothing. The secret is luck, of
course. But you have to learn how to make your
own luck good. Watch carefully, and I'll show you
a real fisherman's little secret." She took a plug
of tobacco out of her pocket, bit off a piece, and
worked it around in her mouth. "Now watch this,"
she said. "This is called magnetizing the hook."

She held up the hook and spit tobacco juice on it. "This always works. Spit on it. Spit is spirit. With tobacco it's a mixture of substance and spirit that gives the hook good luck. The harmony of substance and spirit always brings luck. Never forget it. And if the hook has good luck, so do you."

Ruby Plenty Chiefs, Agnes Whistling Elk, July, and Lynn Andrews
Star Woman

THE GIFT OF LEARNING

IT is a great privilege to be on this earth. It is truly a schoolhouse that we have here for every person alive. Even if they are unaware of that gift, it is the truth and they are learning in spite of themselves. Eventually, all sentient beings may learn what they have come here to learn.

Shakkai
Shakkai, Woman of the Sacred Garden

SEEDS OF CHANGE

Always remember this: It takes only one person to plant the seeds of change. You have as much power to study and learn and work towards meaningful change as anyone else in the world. There is nothing that stands in our way but ourselves.

Lynn Andrews
Coming Full Circle

GATEWAYS

We truly do come onto this earthwalk to become enlightened, and yet it is the one thing that we are most afraid of. Somehow enlightenment implies change. But in that change we are full of terror. When we are faced with something new, something that we have to shift and change to see more clearly, we are afraid to move. Move your eyes in a different direction, the direction of spirit, of sacredness, of walking through the gateway with a new ability for expression, a new contract and relationship with your sacred will.

Lynn Andrews
Woman at the Edge of Two Worlds

EYES OF A ROCK

I am saying that rocks can see you. Rocks are in the mind of the Great Spirit. If you had eyes like the stones, you could explore the universe and both the future and the past. Yes, you could go back into ancient times. If I were to tell you that the stones have seen all of knowledge, to you it would sound absurd. Yet that is true, and they are waiting to reveal their secrets. There are rocks that have eyes that can show you treasures more precious than anything you've ever seen.

Agnes Whistling Elk
Flight of the Seventh Moon

RAINBOW BEAUTY

One day Ginevee held up a crystal to the sun and the light reflected through the crystal, creating prisms of rainbow light that flashed across the ground. She said, "There, crystals are like humans. It is the flaw within that crystal that is creating the rainbow beauty that you see reflected on the ground. It is within our flaws that our beauty comes. Honor your flaws. Celebrate them. They mark your path on this earthwalk. These flaws of yours create the beauty that you are trying to find."

Ginevee and Lynn Andrews
Writing Spirit

REMEMBER WHO YOU ARE

This lifetime is a great gift to any soul. The possibility of enlightenment is within reach of any of us in any lifetime we choose. We are here to learn, wake up, and find the essence of one's spirit—remember who we are. Only through the trials of a challenged life will we grow into a state of perfection.

Lynn Andrews
Dark Sister

ENLIGHTENED EVOLUTION

Have you ever asked yourself how animals evolve?
How does a two-toed horse become a three-toed
horse? By running faster each day than it's capable
of running. We as humans evolve by stretching and
becoming more than we ever dreamed we could be.
So we must heal our fear of taking our power.
The well-being of our world depends on it.

Lynn Andrews
Love and Power

REVERENCE

If you are afraid of death, you will not live your life. You will be immersed in your addictions to fears, to phantoms of the night.

Ani
Windhorse Woman

<u>MIRAGE</u>

"When you met the ghost dolls last night, you experienced the reality of your own individuality. You even saw your worthiness on earth, didn't you?" Agnes said.

"Yes, I felt my significance as a female warrior and my insignificance as another human, and the wonder or the miracle of existence."

Agnes looked off in the distance. She said almost absently, "We are in a mirage of life and death. What is gained is abundant, and what is lost is irretrievable and misplaced utterly."

Agnes Whistling Elk and Lynn Andrews
Star Woman

CENTRAL FLAME

Woman at the Edge of Two Worlds stood before
me in my cave of initiation. "I am the fire," she
said, her face glowing. "I can only move upward as
I burn. You, my daughter, are apprenticed to the
fire. Whether you dreamed of the vast possibility
of transformation or not, your body is now your
teacher. Feel the burn of the heat and welcome
the fire, for the fire is I, the goddess woman who
changes you and prepares you for your sacred
life. Gather knowledge about yourself and your
body. This knowledge is the wood for
your central flame."

**Woman at the Edge of Two Worlds
and Lynn Andrews**
Woman at the Edge of Two Worlds

SPIDER WOMAN'S WEB

Your work makes huge ripples all along the consciousness of human beings. Remember that when you jump on one part of Spider Woman's web, that movement, or activity, is felt all the way on the other side of the world. So take responsibility for the way you move in the world, and the light of this great earth changes and becomes brighter.

Lynn Andrews
The Alchemy of the Inner Shift, Online Course

BE STILL AND LISTEN

Earth is the greatest schoolhouse we will ever have
in this life, if we would but learn to listen to her.

Lynn Andrews
Coming Full Circle

CHIPS OFF THE OLD BLOCK

"Crystals are simply the chips off the throne of the Great Spirit," Butterfly Woman said. "We are all one in our sacred wisdom." Then she reached out her arms. They glittered like diamonds and then became like butterfly wings covered with shiny satin colors—blue, red, and gold. She gently fluttered her wings over me and disappeared.

Butterfly Woman and Lynn Andrews
Crystal Woman

THE TREE OF LIFE

I turned to my teacher as I threw supplies into the back of the truck. "Sometimes, Agnes, I simply want to lie down, enveloped in the energy field of the Great Spirit, close my eyes, and listen to his beating heart. I want to feel that sense of oneness with the universe that surrounds me with such joy and purity of power. I understand that as human beings we want something greater than ourselves to be our God, our power. I realize very clearly that the kingdom of the Great Spirit is within me, it's within you, Agnes, and all of us. Inside. We go up to the top of a tree to see a view out across the landscape. And that's what it is—a view across the landscape, isn't it? It doesn't help us get closer to the sky fathers any more than digging a hole gets us close to Mother Earth. The ability to climb up the tree of life, our Tree of Dreams, is inside us all the time, isn't it?"

Agnes Whistling Elk and Lynn Andrews
Tree of Dreams

BE AWARE OF EGO

"I have always been in awe of Sin Corazón,"
I said. "Not afraid of her, because I don't believe
in what she does. But also I find that a sorcerer
never kills you, she makes you kill yourself
with your own terror."

Ruby agreed, as did Agnes.

"But what I see missing in both Red Dog and Sin
Corazón at her darkest is creativity. Why is that?"

"Because," Agnes said, "she was so present
in her darkness."

I thought about that for some time, and then I
realized what she was saying. "You mean she was
so present in her focus to be evil that her ego
became enormous."

**Agnes Whistling Elk, Ruby Plenty Chiefs,
and Lynn Andrews**
Dark Sister

ARE YOU A HERO?

To me, living your own personal truth is what makes a hero. Greatness often lies not just in our achievements but in the obstacles we overcome to get there, the number of times we pick ourselves up off the ground when something doesn't work out, look at what went wrong, and start all over again. As Winston Churchill once said, "Success is going from failure to failure without losing your enthusiasm!"

Lynn Andrews
Coming Full Circle

LIFE IS AN ART

Balance begins in your own circle. Your life
is then an art, and that is the best position
from which to teach.

Agnes Whistling Elk
Star Woman

CONFUSION

"Ah," Jaguar Woman said. "I can see your confusion. Remember, my daughter, that whatever path you tread, perhaps the only evil in this lifetime is confusion. If you are in a war with another being and you fight with the knives of light and darkness, if you pause for one moment in that state of confusion, it may be your last moment because that is the kind of vulnerability that you cannot afford."

Jaguar Woman and Sin Corazón
Dark Sister

BUILDING FENCES

"I have always thought of myself as free. But I do feel restrictions in my life, and those restrictions are mostly self-made. I thought that what keeps me from my freedom are my responsibilities, but then I thought, I have chosen my responsibilities because I have needed something. Is that right, Agnes? I suddenly feel less and less free."

"Yes, Little Wolf, we put fences around our consciousness endlessly, maybe sometimes in the fear that we might be free."

Agnes Whistling Elk and Lynn Andrews
Woman at the Edge of Two Worlds Workbook

MAY

HOLINESS

Pray for the betterment of wrongs that you see all around you, and embrace that which symbolizes the holy paradise on this earth. Walk in beauty all the days of your life.

Lynn Andrews
Sacred Vision Oracle Cards

CELEBRATION

"Agnes," I said, as the two of us walked across a meadow, poplar trees surrounding us. A hawk took flight from one of the higher branches, the morning light striking its harlequin feathers, making them glisten. "It is a wonderment to me—the trees are laughing. Their leaves are quaking, moving, exercising in celebration of their existence. At least it seems that way to me."

"Look at the flowers," Agnes said. "They celebrate, too. Look at their beauty. Look at their excitement as the sunshine nourishes them. You can see it, you can feel it, can't you?"

Agnes Whistling Elk and Lynn Andrews
Tree of Dreams

FACE FEAR

Fear is a tracker. You must never run from fear.
You must face it.

Twin Dreamers
Dreaming Bear Shield, Online Course

SHAMAN UNDERSTANDING

It is my understanding that shamans have communicated throughout human history on higher
levels of consciousness. That is how, in my experience, we have been able as shamans to understand
one another. When I go to aboriginal Australia, I
sit with the shamans there and we need not speak
the same language. We understand one another
instantly. It is in our eyes; it is in our energy fields.
The source of power is always the same. It is from
the firstness of woman, from our great Mother
Earth, the original mother.

Lynn Andrews
Woman at the Edge of Two Worlds

BE STILL

Tears came to my eyes suddenly as I realized that one of the greatest needs of my life has always been to be loved, and I would create situations where there were a lot of people around and much activity, so I never had to experience the stillness of my own spirit. It's one of the great lessons I've learned with Agnes—to learn how to do that, how to sit still, how slowly to peel away the addictions. One of my greatest fears in life is the fear of death, and yet I know that life is a magnificent mystery and death is the flowering of that life, the completion, the goal of this life, not something to fear. And yet, because it's a mystery, because it's something I cannot control, because it's the unknown, I am still afraid. It's something that I will have to experience someday, as we all will.

Lynn Andrews
Woman at the Edge of Two Worlds Workbook

WABI

"Oh, look," Shakkai said, pointing up to the tree above me. I looked and saw several blossoms that a yellow bird had dislodged with its tiny beak come floating down. "Those are wabi," Shakkai said, smiling. "Wabi is explained many ways, by many people. To me it means a gift. At this moment it is the gift of the cherry tree to life, to the spirit on the wind. It is the giving of the masculine soul to the female acceptance of earth."

Shakkai and Lynn Andrews
Shakkai, Woman of the Sacred Garden

MAY 7

ONENESS

There is no separation from anything. The Great
Spirit is not outside of you, somewhere in the great
beyond. The Great Spirit is part of you and within
all of us, just as we are part of the Great Spirit and
the great Oneness of all of life.

Lynn Andrews
Accessing Wisdom, Online Course

THE BIG PICTURE

There is nothing in this life that is not by some grand design. There is always a bigger picture to everything that happens to us, but to think that you or anyone is so important that others' lives would be completely altered for great, long periods of time simply for your instruction is, of course, unthinkable. But it is also true that there is an agreement on other levels of reality made among all the people whom you have ever known throughout your history as a being.

Lynn Andrews
Dark Sister

WEST

In the west on the sacred wheel is the home of transformations, life, death, and rebirth. It is the place of the power of emotions and passions. West is the direction of female energies. It is the realm of water. Dive deep into the energy of the west.

Lynn Andrews

HONOR THE CHILD WITHIN

"When you discern a person who comes into your life," Agnes counseled me, "ask yourself this question: Does this person honor the child within? For then he or she honors the child in the world."

How do you honor the child within yourself?

Agnes Whistling Elk and Lynn Andrews
Protector of the Children Shield, Online Course

MASTERY

Power without love leaves you without any sustaining energy to keep the feeling of power alive. Love is what brings power into the realm of mastery, where balance and harmony become an everyday experience. And it is within the realm of mastery that your life becomes balanced, powerful, and magical. You can learn to experience extraordinary brilliance every day of your life.

Lynn Andrews
Love and Power

WAVES

"Life is like a wave that rolls into shore. Then it floats back and disappears into the greater sea, until it peaks and comes up again with even greater strength. Life and death are like that," Ani whispered.

Ani and Lynn Andrews
Windhorse Woman

CHALLENGE YOURSELF

You are a warrioress, a hunter. You take life's
circumstances as a challenge.

Agnes Whistling Elk
Star Woman

FIND YOUR DANCE

The women of the Sisterhood teach that
to find that balance, we must understand and
work with the natural forces of the entire universe,
which are both male and female.

Lynn Andrews
Coming Full Circle

LIGHT AND DARK

When men and women fall away from their own
vision of sacredness, their culture falls away into
sleep with them. Sacred vision contains the balance
of light and dark.

Butterfly Woman
Jaguar Woman

LEARN TO DISAPPEAR

"She Who Walks With the Wind can find her shadow in the mirrors," Ginevee said. "If you stare into her eyes or the eyes of your own shadow, you can disappear just like she did."

"Disappear?"

"Yes. The quickest way to learn would be to stare into her eyes...if she would teach you. She knows the trail. She knows what you need."

"But I saw a grotesque face."

"That was your own shadow. The secret is recognizing your own shadow and then learning to have a dialogue with it. Then you learn to disappear."

Ginevee and Lynn Andrews
Crystal Woman

STRANGE GATEWAY

I sat in stillness for a long time. The wind had carried me into its song. As it circled about me in an ever-rising tumultuousness, I stayed quiet like a stone in the midst of a sand storm.

Then I heard Mother's soft voice.

"My daughter, the gateway to death is a strange gateway. The will of the Great Spirit is the only power that allows passage. As I once gave you birth, as once you were inside me, now you give birth to me, as I am forever within you."

Lynn Andrews and her mother, Rosalyn Staples
Woman at the Edge of Two Worlds

LISTEN TO THE WORDS

"You don't listen," Agnes said. "Well, sometimes you don't listen. You don't hear the words of transformation. You yourself teach this, little wolf. There are words and experiences that do not originate from your personality, or even from this lifetime. Those words are created by the magic of alchemy and the energies that are brought together to transform. These energies exist to teach us."

Agnes Whistling Elk and Lynn Andrews
Tree of Dreams

WOMAN AND WAR

A woman will survive to be able to protect a belief
structure that usually houses her family, whether it
be a family of ideas or children. So her basis for war
usually is born of fear deep in the primal part of
herself. War, like an idea or a belief system, is man's
greatest addiction and his greatest vulnerability.
A warring human likes to live on the sheer
edge of life and death.

Ginevee
Crystal Woman

WITNESS YOUR ALLY

Remember that your ally is a magnificent inspiration that comes through your passion; it is an energy form that walks within you and will help you find your way. It is the ally that can lead you out of the terrain of darkness if you have followed darkness too far. To take your power is to face, confront, and witness your ally. The ally is asking you to prove yourself. The ally needs to know that you know how to fight and are powerful enough to understand that process. Become conscious of the ally, feel its energy in your body, see your ally, and work with its power.

Lynn Andrews
Writing Spirit

STORY'S END

We walked with our faces to the westerly
wind for some time.

"There have been many views of death," Shakkai
said. "There was a time when we believed that death
would take us to the heavens where the almighty
God would give us eternal bliss. I personally feel
that death is the end of our story of this lifetime,
and it is important to have a feeling about death—
for death, like the end of a book, is a conclusion."

Shakkai and Lynn Andrews
Shakkai, Woman of the Sacred Garden

YOU ARE SPECIAL

Your life has meaning. Your life is special. Your life is like no other. So celebrate the integrity of your own very special personality. Follow your truth and don't be afraid to fail or succeed. If something doesn't work out the way you want it to, stick with it until you find out what went wrong, and then do what you have to do to change it.

Lynn Andrews
Coming Full Circle

NORTH-SOUTH MOVEMENT

When looked at on the Sacred Wheel, the movement in any relationship between east and west promotes understanding and knowledge. But enlightenment and intuition and spirit come from a north-south movement, one that is motivated by your instincts. If you live without the north-south, you feel as if you are losing your soul. You feel like you are dying. There is transformation in movement between north and south, but never between east and west.

Zoila and Lynn Andrews
Star Woman

CENTER YOURSELF

Never leave your center. Count your bad points as well as your good. What is good and what is bad are most often purely relative. If you sense a weakness within yourself, explore it. It may become the source of your greatest strength.

Lynn Andrews
Love and Power

FIRST LESSON OF POWER

"I'm afraid of being different," I said.

"But you've always been different."

"Yes, I guess so."

"Well then?" Ginevee was giggling. "You don't accept who you are. It's a mirage that any of us are alone." Ginevee pointed up to the moon that still shone in the night sky. "The moon is alone shining her wisdom onto Mother Earth and yet she is not alone. She is held onto a path, a transit of the universe by the galaxy that she belongs to. First you must accept that you are utterly alone. That, as you know, is the first lesson of power. And then you must realize that none of us can exist without the other, girl— none of us. We are not separate, we are all part of each other."

Ginevee and Lynn Andrews
Crystal Woman

PURE CREATIVITY

Very gently and quietly, Agnes said, "When you are gone, when you are no more, when you have moved into the beat of the mother drum"—on her drum she began to play a very slow heartbeat— "move your consciousness into the beat of the drum and hear yourself. Hear the Great Spirit speaking to you with wisdom. When you are out of the way, all possibilities are upon you. Teach your apprentices how to remove their conscious mind from their reckoning. Let them bridge directly into what you call the subconscious, into the dream lodges of the universe. Then you are pure creativity, and nothing then is impossible for you."

Agnes Whistling Elk and Lynn Andrews
Dark Sister

WHERE ANGER LIVES

Think about where anger lives in your body. Close
your eyes for a moment and feel where anger,
where holding the word "anger" or the thought
of anger, lives in your body. Then make a mental
note and imprint it on this part of your body. This
is something you want to heal before it grows into
something you do not want in your life. Anger can
be like a flame. It can be the other side of passion,
motivating you. Or it can paralyze you completely.
The choice is yours. Neither your anger nor what
it was that made you so angry has anything to do
with how you choose to respond to your anger.
Think about it.

Lynn Andrews
Coming Full Circle

LOVE ALL THAT IS

Your life is a sacred bundle made up of love and
your dreams. You become what you think and
dream. If you love all that is, you become the
Great Mystery in all things.

Lynn Andrews
Sacred Vision Oracle Cards

FEEL THE MAGIC

"You have a way of seeing and feeling magic,"
Agnes said. "But to feel that magic, you have to be
whole, and your spirit has to live inside you.
It cannot be lent out in little pieces to anyone else.
You can share your love, but you cannot
share your spirit."

Agnes Whistling Elk and Lynn Andrews
Tree of Dreams

ENDURING

If you can become like a stone, you will experience the stillness of the stones, and then the flower of your spirit will brighten into full bloom with patience and enduring grace.

Lynn Andrews
The Power Deck

DON'T GET CAUGHT IN THE DREAM

"There is no telling why the Great Spirit works in such mysterious ways. That is what makes life so powerful a challenge for learning, if only you can see that the forks in the trail are opportunities." Agnes grinned at me. "Little wolf, don't get caught in the dream. Don't misunderstand what you are seeing!"

Agnes Whistling Elk and Lynn Andrews
Dark Sister

AN EVOLVED BEING

Agnes looked at me and said, "Lynn, now you know the reason you are on this good Mother Earth. Now you know why you chose the parents that you chose. You chose them to give you the problems or gifts that you have in this lifetime. They gave you a set of emotional problems that you need to solve and to understand. As a result of that, you will become much closer to being an enlightened woman. When you can live in happiness and joy and peace instead of tension and chaos and pain and terror, when you can choose happiness on the other side of the abyss from where you stood while growing up, you will be an evolved being. You will have done the work you have come into this lifetime to do."

Agnes Whistling Elk and Lynn Andrews
Windhorse Woman

SPIRIT IS FOOD

"Fears always manifest themselves to the one who creates them. I can see when your spirit is food and what entity is eating you. You have many fears around you, and that is why you are so heavy. Without your food—gift of energy—the entity would waste away and perish."

Agnes Whistling Elk and Lynn Andrews
Jaguar Woman

<u>WAKING UP</u>

Never forget that life is a process of waking up
from a long and ancient sleep of the soul.
Each of us has to fill up the emptiness
inside us in different ways.

Agnes Whistling Elk
Dark Sister

RELATIONSHIPS

Every relationship is a world unto itself. Each of
us gives a unique meaning to every relationship we
have, whether sacred, family, lover, country, society, humanity and all that lives. Discover the truth
in your commitments and the love in your personal
agreements. Each of us gives a message to the world
when we are born. Discover what relationship and
healing you chose as a message to yourself for
your own healing.

Lynn Andrews

FEEL THE WIND

Always remember this: no matter what you do, the
Great Spirit has a hand on your back, breathing
the power of truth through the wind. So when you
are struggling, remember to breathe. Feel the wind,
the breath of the Great Spirit at your back.
Breathe in deeply and draw strength,
for you are taking in the breath of God.

Lynn Andrews
Coming Full Circle

THE WEIGHT OF THE WORLD

Agnes reached out her hand and touched my shoulder and said, "Lynn, these shoulders carry the weight of the world. Women carry the weight of the world. It is a heavy weight, because from the day you were born, you knew how to See. You could see the pain in the world, and you wanted to do something about it. You cared. Women care. They want to nurture the earth back to health."

Agnes Whistling Elk and Lynn Andrews
Dark Sister

DREAM WORLD

"Are you saying that we all live in our
own dream world?" I said.

"Yes, but what happens if I show you how to move
your essence into another form? What good is that
in your particular world? How can that help you?"
Twin Dreamers asked.

"I am not sure."

"Truly, the only wisdom to understand is that
each mind is a world unto itself."

"Then if I no longer see the dream,
I no longer see the world."

"That's right. So then, how do you live?"

"Do you mean how do I live without form?"

"Yes. You are accustomed to the false dream of form, duality, and separation."

"Would I disappear?"

"Only if you chose to disappear."

Twin Dreamers and Lynn Andrews
Star Woman

BE OF SERVICE

"But to learn, Ruby," I said, "sometimes you have to wrap around something to learn it, don't you?"

"There are two ways to wrap around something. One way is to suck it dry like a parasite that lives off of its host until the host is dead. And then what does it have? Nothing. It usually dies. That's one way. The other way is to be of service."

"What's the difference?" I asked.

"Service," Ruby said, leaning forward a bit to make sure I was listening carefully, "is not servitude. As you become an apprentice, you begin to anticipate what I need, and in this way you yourself become the teacher. You think about what I told you, and about everything you've learned so far, so that you can be of service to me. In that way you learn what the teacher is made of. And when you learn that, then you've learned the lesson. Then I am free and you are free, and we walk away from each other in love, in complete autonomy and freedom, but in complete service to one another. There is community, in a sense, between us. We love each other, we care for each other, but we are free from each other. You are not dependent on my life force, little wolf, and I am not dependent on yours. Service is how you begin to understand personal power."

Ruby Plenty Chiefs and Lynn Andrews
Tree of Dreams

POOR COW

"Remember the story of Poor Cow, Lynn," Agnes said. "He was a warrior. But he would go through the village and say, 'Poor little White Fawn. She hasn't had enough to eat. Oh, poor Little Crow. He has a sore leg. Oh, poor me. I have lost my shadow.' One day the medicine woman came to him and said, 'Poor Cow, you need to go into the sweat lodge and pray and maybe then you can find your shadow.' When he came out, he was a completely different person. He no longer felt sorry for everyone, including himself. He was healed."

"Agnes, that is a good story for this time in our history. We forget why we're here. We get so immersed in our sadness. We forget that we are here to be enlightened."

Agnes Whistling Elk and Lynn Andrews
Medicine Woman

YOUR CHOICES DEFINE YOU

Anger is going to come up in our lives. Things happen and they aren't always pleasant. When anger
comes, you can make good use of it or you can fall
prey to it and become its victim. It is a choice that
is yours to make every time something angers you.

Lynn Andrews
Coming Full Circle

GIVE BACK TO THE SPIRIT
OF THE PLANTS

When you approach all of life as a prayer for the
magnificence and the miracle of life, then when
you are working in your garden or preparing vegetables to be eaten, you understand that through
what you are doing, your presence transforms
life. You talk to the plants that provide the fruits
and vegetables of your sustenance. Those plants
are alive, they have a spirit, and when you eat the
plant, it gives away the power from its spirit to you.
You give back to the spirit of the plant through
prayers of thanks.

Lynn Andrews

EXTRAORDINARY ACCOMPLISHMENTS

To celebrate what you have accomplished in your life, to celebrate who you are, what the meaning of your life is, is to stand in the moment, in the center, equidistant from all positions on the perimeter of your sacred circle and proclaim to the world that you are something special, that you have survived in a way that has promoted your life and the life of others. We are, all of us, extraordinary powerful beings who through our love for the goodness of the universe and the light that lives within each of us have survived. And we should be ultimately proud of that extraordinary accomplishment.

Lynn Andrews
Woman at the Edge of Two Worlds Workbook

FIND THE SECRET WITHIN

"At one point our destiny becomes clear. I think that our lives are like that. The secret is being born within you. There is a kind of truth ahead of you, black wolf, a truth that you have not seen before."

"How do I find it?" I asked. "Please, Agnes, talk to me. I can't stand the suspense."

"It is something to be discovered, and you will. You have a life that is well examined and you often ask questions that are unanswerable. But you are going to find the scent. And then, as abruptly as the wind changes, you will see the changes that will affect you forever. Those changes have to do with your depth of love, including all that you have thought was your destiny. And then the disturbance you feel now will lift, as if taken by spirits in the night. In the morning glow, you will not be so heavy anymore."

Agnes Whistling Elk and Lynn Andrews
Tree of Dreams

OPEN YOUR HEART

"If you can find truly deep feelings in your life, your creativity is expanded. If you find relationships in your environment that open your heart, you can recreate those feelings once you know the trail. Once you know the trail, you can find herbs that can marry you, that can give you a quality of life that is very different from what you ordinarily experience."

"Is that where homeopathy and flower essences come from? Is that the origin of the idea of healing with such elements?" I asked.

"Yes, it is. It has to do with the frequency in your body. It is really very simple. Shamans around the world for all time have known these secrets to be true and have healed with them throughout the ages."

Shakkai and Lynn Andrews
Shakkai, Woman of the Sacred Garden

YOUR PATH OF POWER

I am a warrior of the light,
I live the integrity of that truth with great care,
From a center within myself that is pure
goodness—
The embodiment of the peaceful soul.

Lynn Andrews
The Power Deck

WIND IS SPIRIT

Allow yourself to move out into nature and see the light on the trees, hear the sounds of the birds and the wind. Wind is spirit. Which wind direction is your ally? Is it the west wind or the north wind, the south wind or the east? They all mean something different. What do they mean to you? The west wind and the clouds can help you in your dreaming. When you sit somewhere under a tree and watch the clouds moving slowly above you, you can imagine with the power of your mind and the power of your heart and the power of your dreaming body what it would be like to be floating on those clouds. Begin to dance with that feeling. Live with it. Join it.

Lynn Andrews
Writing Spirit

BEGINNING, MIDDLE, END

"When you write a story, you have a beginning, a middle, and an end," Shakkai said, "and you progress toward a certain tension at different points in the writing of that book, all of which is put into perspective by the end of the book. That is just as it is in life. Our feelings about death give us a point of view, a stance in life as a warrior of the spirit."

Shakkai and Lynn Andrews
Shakkai, Woman of the Sacred Garden

FIRST, LOVE YOURSELF

To truly have power, you must first love yourself enough to stay in your own center of truth. Once we have embraced love as a feeling about ourselves for ourselves, it will never go away. It becomes a state of being and is maintained by the constant awareness of keeping our heart open to ourselves and others.

Lynn Andrews
Love and Power

HAPPY HUNTING

Don't allow anyone to ruin the happy hunting territories of your own mind. A happy frame of mind is your food. Protect her. Go where there is fresh grass and clear water. Where the game is plentiful to hunt.

Agnes Whistling Elk
Star Woman

COLLECTION

As your spirit shield flies through the universe, collecting the dusts of creation and experience, there is always an agreement. There is something to be learned so that the spirit shield can be imprinted with even more power and evolvement. So to think that your spirit shield is spinning away into worlds of light and darkness without thought, without direction, without there being the powers of the gods and the goddesses surrounding you, is folly.

Jaguar Woman
Dark Sister

SUMMER

Summer is the season when flowers bloom, when fruits and vegetables ripen on the vine. It is the time when farmers must tend to their crops closely, pruning away the excess growth and those branches that are not growing properly so that the life of the plant is not drained away. Don't forget about the summertime of our projects, the critical time of cultivating and nurturing what we've planted, even those parts of our lives that are most important to us. Take good care of the things you start. Take good care of the people in your life. Let those you love know how much you appreciate them by nurturing them in a special way.

Lynn Andrews
Coming Full Circle

YOUR SONG LINE

You have a destiny. It may feel obscured or
untouchable at times, but rest assured that it is
always with you. Your song line is safe in your
heart; you need only stop to connect with it.
Do you sense your beautiful light—the spark
that never dies?

Lynn Andrews
Sacred Vision Oracle Cards

PANNING FOR GOLD

You know how to pan for gold. You observe a person, listen deeply, then jiggle that pan, and you wait for the sand to settle and the water to clear. You watch that, symbolically, in other people. You talk to the gas station attendant. You talk to the guy in the hardware store. You talk to the person who fixes your car. And you ask questions while moving into that place of the void instantly. You know that everyone has gold inside them—a spark of light—if you can just find it. The Great Spirit lives in everything and everyone. There's gold in all of life and in each of us.

Face in the Water
Tree of Dreams

MOVE INTO YOUR DREAM LODGE

"Lynn, teach your apprentices how to remove their conscious mind from their reckoning. Let them bridge directly into what you call the subconscious, into the dream lodges of the universe. Then you are pure creativity, and nothing then is impossible for you. You are capable of writing the greatest novel, able to conjure the most healing ceremony to present to your people. Beauty surrounds you. Light becomes your servant as you become the servant of light."

Agnes Whistling Elk and Lynn Andrews
Dark Sister

THE SACRED NOW

"The sorcerer, or the magician, knows the Sacred Now. The source of that kind of now is illusion. As a shaman you dwell in the almost fatal crack between light and darkness where the beings of mystery swim in unknown rivers of energy. As a shaman you're like the cosmic architect building dams made of prayer sticks and lightning rods and you alter the shape and course of those rivers of energy. That is the power of creation. That too is a world of life and death and great danger. And that experience is in the Sacred Now."

Ginevee and Lynn Andrews
Crystal Woman

I AM AT PEACE AND ALL IS WELL

The shamanism of the Sisterhood of the Shields is the shamanism of the sacred warrioress, the spiritual warrior who knows that Mother Earth gives us life force, the life blood of our sacred body, and that the plants and animals, the four-leggeds, fish and winged ones, give us nourishment and healing both in the physical realm and in the realm of spirit as we ride the windhorse of our sacred intent into a world of harmony and light. As spiritual warriors, we do commerce in the world with the integrity of our own life and spirit. Our weapons are the shields of awareness, personal integrity, the symbols of ancient truth, and the sacred give-away.

Lynn Andrews
Coming Full Circle

SPIRIT INTO SUBSTANCE
INTO SPIRIT

Zoila leaned back on her blanket for a contemplative moment. She said, "Men and women need to find something that involves the manifestation of spirit into substance and substance back into spirit."

"How about writing?" I said.

"Yes. Writing could be very good. You bring an idea in the form of spirit and intuition down from the north and manifest it in a physical book. You write physically. It reaches out to people on an intuitional level, and you receive substance— that is to say, money—in payment."

Zoila and Lynn Andrews
Star Woman

MANIFEST YOUR TRUTH

If you could make one act of power that would change your life forever, what do you think it would be? An act of power is an act that is performed from your strongest passion, out of the depths of your being. An act of power is an accurate manifestation of your personal truth in the world around you. For an act of power, you focus all of your desire and all of your energy, and put it into one single endeavor. An act of power is the visible and artful manifestation of your truth in the world. An act of power is when you take all of your focus, all of your energy, and all of your love, and put it into one endeavor with passion.

Lynn Andrews
Love and Power

UNUSUAL ABILITIES

All plants have talents. Some can be used to heal
bruises, some can lower a temperature, some can
intoxicate you, and so forth. That is their ability
and their purpose on earth. We are different than
plants. A plant knows what its life is about from
the moment it sprouts as a seedling. We humans,
on the other hand, are only a possibility when
we are born. We must discover our purpose and
meaning and then we must find the courage
to follow that purpose.

Agnes Whistling Elk
Crystal Woman

WALK IN BALANCE

"When you have experienced the ceremony that the Sisterhood has prepared for you, Lynn, you will then be able to take what you have learned back to your people, who so desperately need to walk in balance, with one foot in the physical and one foot in spirit. They have lost their spiritual understanding, they have lost their sacred vision, and so many of your people have lost their spirit. But you will help lead your sisters back to the source of their own truth."

Agnes Whistling Elk and Lynn Andrews
Woman at the Edge of Two Worlds

A SECRET

"I do have a secret," Agnes said, placing her hand over her heart. The turquoise green of her bracelet of looped beads matched the colors in the shallow part of the creek water. "My secret is hidden in the lightning and the thunder. It has a color, but it is the color of our remembering—our remembering from a far history," Agnes said, looking toward the horizon. "We have created landscapes together in our work, and we have seen mountains and rivers and events that have imprinted our souls and burned our eyes. What we choose to ignore in life changes us and makes us prisoners of what we refuse to see. But do not despair, because we are moving into a time of new form. We are, piece by piece, through disintegration and the friction of heat and creativity, living in a great time of change. Maybe we won't learn the secret on a conscious level, but we are still becoming that secret."

Agnes Whistling Elk and Lynn Andrews
Tree of Dreams

MALE AND FEMALE

In the shamanic worldview every person has both a male and a female aspect to their being. Both are integral, inextricable parts of the essence of who we are. The feminine side of our nature is introspective. It is receptive, capable of going within to dream and receive the great wisdom of our consciousness. The masculine side teaches us how to organize our consciousness. It is the masculine side that teaches us how to express our dreams and bring an exchange of energy back from the world, such as money or food or other material goods necessary to our survival. We need both to survive, thrive, and flourish.

Lynn Andrews

THE LODGE OF BALANCE

Harmony lives in the lodge of balance and involves
equilibrium between the physical and spiritual
aspects of your life. For there to be harmony, there
must be balance.

Lynn Andrews
The Power Deck

WE ARE RESPONSIBLE

"The spirits of the mountain have presented you
with a test. Power is located in your will," Ani said,
placing her flattened hand on my solar plexus.
"Creative acts manifest through the use of will.
Pure will is what is bringing about the change."

"What do you mean 'change'?"

"The process that we call life is going through a
great shift. We experience that shift in terms of
energy. Energy is building now in all of its forms.
It means that we are all responsible for all
the reality that surrounds us."

Ani and Lynn Andrews
Windhorse Woman

SPIRIT POWER

"You remember, Lynn," Agnes said, "never throw sand in the eyes of the buffalo before you kill it. A shaman woman is made just like you are made of other life-forms. You take spirit power from those life-forms and you are made into an extraordinary being that is comprised of parts of all living things. You experience all life and then you can heal all life as it heals you."

Agnes Whistling Elk and Lynn Andrews
Crystal Woman

NEVER FEAR

Darkness is the norm, and there is nothing to fear.
The way is lit with moments of enlightenment.

Lynn Andrews
Sacred Vision Oracle Cards

TEAR AWAY THE VEILS

"The Great Spirit has been trying to enlighten the beings of this earth for all time. It is a very difficult task as well you know, my daughter. When you tear away a veil of ignorance from someone's vision, another one replaces it. It seems that we never get anywhere. As we move through this existence, problems beset us at every turn. For many years I felt the tragedy of this in my heart, and I was filled with anger and I fought side by side with my people for our lost borders, for the land that is our Great Mother. I could not understand why the surveyors came into my cabin when I was so young and raped me and put out my eyes with the points of their compass so that I could not identify them. I didn't want to live. You have heard this story before. But remember that I understand your feelings of terror and sadness and your feelings of frustration, for we have all felt them. But there comes a time when you begin to understand the greater patterns in life, the energy flows."

Ruby lifted her hands and caressed the currents of air around her.

"We are involved in a sacred dance. We have chosen this dance. We have given over our lives to the preservation of life force and the goodness that exists within each human being."

Ruby Plenty Chiefs and Lynn Andrews
Shakkai, Woman of the Sacred Garden

CROSSROADS

Sit in the center of your own circle of power and
explore the directions of your life, explore your
shields, explore the crossroads that you sit in
at this moment in time.

Jaguar Woman
Dark Sister

STRUCTURE

"You know what's going to heal the earth," Agnes said. "So structurally, if your bones are telling you that you need to pay attention to structure, that you need to pay attention to how you have ordered your life in a structural way, then do so. Don't give up. Don't round your shoulders and apologize for who you are. Take strength. Pick up your lance and move out into the world from a sacred stance. Know that the strength is in there. The warrior stands within you and announces to the world that you are not to be fooled with, that you are a good enemy, and you will give them a good fight to the death, if needed. Then your bones will be healed."

Agnes Whistling Elk and Lynn Andrews
Woman at the Edge of Two Worlds

REJOICE

We are made from the stars, and to the stars we must one day return. Rejoice! You are upward growing. You are entwined with all the flowers of the worlds. Follow the healing melody of your highest dreams and leave behind the souls that know no rest.

Lynn Andrews
Sacred Vision Oracle Cards

PADDLE WITH THE FLOW

When you move through life with a conscious
awareness of earth's rhythms, you move into the
flow of energy as it courses throughout the entire
universe. That is when you have true power working with you and all of possibility is at your
fingertips, as opposed to paddling blindly upstream
the way modern people tend to do.

Lynn Andrews
Coming Full Circle

STALKING

You have circled and stalked all your life to understand and change the conditioning that holds
you back from knowing and expressing your true
self and the great joy and vision with which you
were born into this world. Healing from the conditioning and changing your patterns takes time,
repetition, and remaining committed to your
intent. But the breakthrough comes, and one
day you wake up in your authentic self,
and you know it to be true.

Lynn Andrews
Hero of the Dream, Online Course

YOU ARE EXTRAORDINARY

Your life is an extraordinary tree, the flowering of
which is really the process of death. Death is the
opening and the ushering of your spirit into the
greater mystery, which makes all of life understand-
able, but to get to that point there are plateaus.
These plateaus are celebrations for what you have
become, your sacred lodge of the self.

Lynn Andrews
Woman at the Edge of Two Worlds Workbook

WAKE UP

Be sensitive to the process of awareness. Wake up
to your senses and feel the coolness of a breeze on
your skin like silk. Be aware of other people's needs
as well as your own.

Lynn Andrews
Love and Power

JULY 15

AWAKEN THE SPIRITS

"The spirits sleep in all the named and nameless things. They are fast asleep in everything. Yet there may not have been a ceremony here for the last thousand years. To us it seems like a long time, but it is but a breath in forever. The spirits of this power place wait and they slumber. When you, as a shaman, arrive, the first thing you must do is wake up the spirits and make them stand up. Remember that a ceremony is only as powerful as the person giving it. If you can't wake up the spirits of a place, you may as well pack it in and go home."

"Tell me what to do, Twin Dreamers."

"Your bundle is open. Call to the spirits to awaken!"

Twin Dreamers and Lynn Andrews
Star Woman

MOVE WITH THE FLOW

Learning to move with the flow of power and
energy in the universe instead of against it is very
different from moving with the flow of the crowd.
When you learn to move with the flow of power
and energy in the universe, you learn about
yourself and your own relationship with power.
You learn to dream for yourself and to honor your
own dreams in this world without harming other
people or this great earth in the process.

Lynn Andrews
Spirit Dreaming, Online Course

EXPERIENCE, NOT WORDS

"Your story has been told, my daughter, and it has been laid to rest. This story has been difficult and it has been hard for you many long time. For many people, life is like sitting on the edge of this spring, for they never once enter the water. Your people, they know the words. Because they know the words, they think they have had the experience. The story you have lived with me has been mysterious and you have found your way through much darkness. But you have experienced these things and in the end your experience is all you have. You have learned well a good lesson," Ginevee said touching my hand.

Ginevee and Lynn Andrews
Crystal Woman

NO FALSE PRIDE

"What if someone insults you and hurts you?"
I asked Agnes.

"A warrioress always needs a challenge. Why is it
that a person is able to insult you? What's going on
with your misdirected pride? If we blow ourselves
up in this manner, we are meat for any insult. But
if we are not puffed up with pride, very little can
hurt us." She laughed. "Besides, with no false pride,
you are a smaller target."

Agnes Whistling Elk and Lynn Andrews
Star Woman

YOUR MYTHOLOGY

"Spider Woman, I have been having dreams about Red Dog. And dreams about you. Is that why you have come?" I asked.

"Yes, and I am here because there is something that you need to learn. You are facing your own mortality. That is disturbing for you. There are many places in our lives where we create a mythology about who we are. There are intimate relations that sometimes don't work, and when they fail, we go out into society and find new intimate relationships. We go back and forth in our lives, back and forth, wondering if we will ever find happiness. This is the essence of our existence, the beginning, middle, and end."

Spider Woman and Lynn Andrews
Tree of Dreams

THE UNKNOWABLE

"Black wolf, remember the sacred spiral. At the center is the formless unknowable. The center represents your shaman death where you finally let go of the lodges of the mind and ego and our relative sense of time. The power of the unknowable is leaning on you. You are beginning to feel her presence in your life."

Ruby Plenty Chiefs and Lynn Andrews
Crystal Woman

THE SACRED FEMININE

It is through the sacred feminine that we access the sacred dream for our lives. This is the great dream that was formed when you sat with the Great Spirit and all of the masters and beings of light in the universe before you were born, discovering what lessons you needed to learn during this lifetime so that you could reach towards enlightenment, our spirit's destination.

Grandmother and Lynn Andrews
The Woman of Wyrrd

REFLECTION ON WHO YOU ARE

"All of life is a circle, Lynn. All beings that are alive are part of that circle. Though we become lost in the dream of duality, the dream of separateness, we are in fact all reflections of the Great Spirit."

"So you are saying that we are all part of the same spirit and the same God," I said.

"Yes, we are indeed all one. We cannot lose each other on any level, but sometimes in our ignorance we forget the meaning of life, and we forget our destiny. What we do together is a process of remembering, of remembering who we truly are."

Agnes Whistling Elk and Lynn Andrews
Medicine Woman

LOVE IS EVERYWHERE

Our thoughts are but forms of energy. What you
think, you become. So watch what you think and
celebrate your own truth in everything that you
do. Become a hero to yourself, and your world will
always be filled with heroes.

Lynn Andrews
Coming Full Circle

AN ADVENTURE OF SPIRIT

"The female warrior knows that life is an adventure of the spirit," Twin Dreamers said. "She knows that this earthwalk is only a dream born of a greater dream beyond our imagination."

Twin Dreamers and Lynn Andrews
Star Woman

TWIN DREAMERS

Twin Dreamers is a woman who behaves almost without restraint. I don't mean without responsibility; I mean without limits in regards to what a woman is supposed to do or not supposed to do. She goes beyond the limits of even ordinary reality, because she is a shape shifter and helps you to experience her in different form—maybe very young or old, maybe as a hawk. She can move wherever she wishes. It is her power, and she has cultivated that power.

Lynn Andrews
Woman at the Edge of Two Worlds

BE UNASSUMMING

"You see, Lynn, if you could teach your apprentices to simply be unassuming of their knowledge, then they can learn and work. And yet, the ego moves into the place of love and kicks love out. That sorcerer tries to keep you from the top of the mountain. That sorcerer is the ego, always and at last, the position of fear. It inspires fear; that sorcerer. It tries to make you afraid of going any further. If you get twisted up in the drama that people create, you get lost in a darkness. And heaven knows, you lose that vulnerability, that place of opening where you can help someone."

Ruby Plenty Chiefs and Lynn Andrews
Tree of Dreams

IT'S ALL ABOUT TIMING

Timing, your ability to know when to hold and when to let go, is one of the essentials of a masterful life—knowing when to move, knowing when to let go of a stock before it plummets, knowing when to release, knowing when to buy, when to hold. If you love yourself, then you can love others and release them as necessary. Letting go of friends and situations is often the hardest task, but often the kindest in the long run. If you can sense when to let go of situations that drain you and no longer serve anyone, you hold the key that unlocks the door to true skill and mastery of the tools of power.

Lynn Andrews
Love and Power

MIRRORS FOR GROWTH

"Shakkai, the ancient teachings talk about the act of power and how important that is to provide mirrors for growth."

"Yes," Shakkai said, "An act of power is very important, but remember, you can only give up something that you have, and if you do not have an act of power, you cannot give it up."

Shakkai and Lynn Andrews
Shakkai, Woman of the Sacred Garden

THE GIFT OF COMPLETION

I realize that in loving someone, I will complete myself within the oneness of all of life. The most extraordinary gift is what only I can give, and it is important to honor how that gift changes someone. In keeping my heart open, I help those I love to enter into situations and experiences they would never have seen or felt on their own.

Lynn Andrews
Dark Sister

THE GREAT TREES ARE FALLING

I was watching the light play across the desert at sunset. Before me was a great, tall saguaro cactus that had been living for hundreds of years. Cochise and Geronimo lived and died in its shade. But I noticed that it was leaning dangerously to the left. Even so, at the very top the cactus was birthing new arms that were stretching up toward the sun. It bloomed gorgeous pink flowers. How like our society! We bloom with abundance and color and spiritual idealism—all the while seemingly unaware, like the saguaro cactus, that our roots are rotting underneath us from a lack of care and the deadly infiltration of what is unfamiliar and can destroy us. If we do not become aware of our totality, top to bottom, we may fall and die.

Lynn Andrews

I EXPRESS MY ACTIVITY

Being grateful is a celebration of the life force. It is a celebration of light, a way of saying to the Great Spirit, "Thank you for the great gifts of life. Thank you for all of the things that have gone right in my life today," instead of, "Blast the world for all of the things that have gone wrong."

Lynn Andrews
Coming Full Circle

AUGUST

OUR BODY OF MEMORIES

Remember that muscles hold memory, that the muscles of our bodies are the source of a great deal of inspiration. We think that inspiration comes only from the ethers, but often it comes from the memories that are held in our bodies.

Lynn Andrews
Standing at the Crossroads of Upheaval,
Online Course

PRIMAL POWER

The primal power of the source of wisdom is held
and carried by woman. It takes the receptivity of
woman, of the sacred void, to open yourself to the
primal power of all things. The womb of Mother
Earth gives birth to all women.

Lynn Andrews
Shakkai, Woman of the Sacred Garden

<u>RELEASE</u>

Even when you have endured a great confrontation,
remember the strength of relationship to spirit,
the whole. The true self is one of release—a soul
unbound by the earthly and ready to fly.

Lynn Andrews
Sacred Vision Oracle Cards

FOLLOW YOUR INNER BEAUTY

Your path in life up to this moment has been to
always be quite public with your feelings and who
you are. You could say that it's as if somebody had
turned your pockets inside out. Be careful that that
does not become your shape. Nothing is wrong in
people knowing who you are and in talking about
following your dreams so that other people will
have the courage to do the same. But all that is
exquisite in life is inner. It is inside you,
and that means that it is also very
private to you and to you alone.

Agnes Whistling Elk
Tree of Dreams

INVISIBILITY

We are sorcerers of the light, not of the darkness. A dark sorcerer is invisible because he does not want to be seen doing his dirty work. We are invisible at times because we are building our strength and our power to enhance the life that we live. How do you enhance your life? What invisible aspects of your character do you treasure that sometimes you keep very private and to yourself?

Lynn Andrews
Woman at the Edge of Two Worlds Workbook

PAST, PRESENT, FUTURE

Move into the different dimensions of life, into
the different dimensions of consciousness. Learn
to move into those dimensions not just in spirit,
but with your body as well. There are other levels
of consciousness going on with what you are doing
right now, other lifetimes that you might want to
experience. Those are two bookend experiences,
because one is past and one is future.

Lynn Andrews

CLOSE UP DEAD

"As Ginevee used to tell you," Agnes put in, "you are close up dead sometimes. What she meant is that sometimes you do not look into all aspects of yourself. It's very important to look at all of your anxieties and impulses. Oftentimes, they lead you into dark places. Darkness does define the light"— Agnes pointed to the sky outside the window—"just as that magnificent black horizon is defined by the light of the moon."

Agnes Whistling Elk and Lynn Andrews
Dark Sister

ECSTATIC DREAM

I was mesmerized by the beauty before me.
I looked up into the tree branches and caught
glimpses of shimmering black and orange satin and
tiny sheets of velvety red turning to peacock blue.
The tree had taken on another life, a release into its
own ecstatic dream—its shape being carried away
on fluttering wings.

Lynn Andrews
Jaguar Woman

BRING IN SPIRIT

Life is the process of movement. And enlightenment is found in the movement between
inspiration and the manifestation of that inspiration. Bringing spirit into your physical life and
manifesting your intuitions from spirit creates
your art, money, movement, and success.

Lynn Andrews
Love and Power

POSSIBILITIES

"Everything is made of Power, Lynn," Agnes said.
"But if you ignore that possibility, that knowledge
is wasted and is of no use to you."

Agnes Whistling Elk and Lynn Andrews
Crystal Woman

BEING HUMAN

Observe your own behavior. Look down on yourself like a noble eagle in the sky. See how foolish you are, and forgive yourself. You are only human. See what the thunder chiefs see. Against the grandeur of the sky we all shrink in importance.

Agnes Whistling Elk
Star Woman

STAND IN YOUR TRUTH

"There are times when you must learn to fight,"
Shakkai said, "because we are human, and out of
the ignorance of being human there are times when
people will be angered by your goodness and your
light, and they will try to defeat you, but you have
to stand in your own truth. You know about your
integrity. You know that what you are doing is true
and right in the world. And that's, in a sense, all
you have, and no one can take away what you are.
No one."

Shakkai and Lynn Andrews
Shakkai, Woman of the Sacred Garden

MY HEART IS OPEN

I learned that if you want to have power in your
life, you must make a place within you for power
to live. You do that by letting go of your neediness,
the need for someone else to make things
happen for you.

Lynn Andrews
Coming Full Circle

TIE NEW KNOTS

"I taught you something new, and that is the trail out of depression. When you work with people who are troubled, teach them something new. Not only does it bring them out of a destructive mood, but it centers them. It changes them, like poetry, like a beautiful work of art. When a shaman works with you, he or she works on the tapestry of your life, helping you tie new knots, bring in new colors to your design, and when that happens, your heart opens and all of life becomes possible again."

Agnes Whistling Elk and Lynn Andrews
Shakkai, Woman of the Sacred Garden

DREAMTIME DESIGNS

"If you see clearly it will come true. What you design in your inner life will manifest in your outer life. See, it is all here on your sacred stone. These markings are the designs of your tiniest cells that make up your body. These designs are also the sacred pattern of your destiny. Never forget what is here in the Dreamtime."

Oruncha and Lynn Andrews
Crystal Woman

ORACLE

Inside every person is an oracle. Perhaps you want to learn something on a given day. Maybe you're out in the middle of the desert. You don't have your teachers around. You have only someone checking groceries in a grocery store, let's say. You go in, you talk to them. You ask them a question that comes to you from your body-mind, from your spirit. That evokes a response. They may not even know what they are saying. But the Great Spirit speaks to you through them, through their knowledge, that perhaps they don't even know they're in touch with. It changes them. It gives them something, and it gives you a magic moment that enters you and brings you light.

Ruby Plenty Chiefs
Tree of Dreams

LEARN TO READ ENERGY

This earthwalk is a teaching about the dance of energies. All energies speak to one another in some way. Energy follows thought. We feel energy shifts in other parts of the world as surely as you feel the warm wind on your face now. You must learn to use your own body to read energy.

Agnes Whistling Elk
Crystal Woman

FIND YOUR DREAMS

As above, so below. It is simple: it takes absolute
intent from your open heart. Feel not the rain, but
seek the serenity of love. Love truly is the healing
element of our world. Allow yourself to dream now
of a life of learning, wisdom, and reflection.

Amina
Coming Full Circle

A FINELY TUNED BEING

It is good to focus your attention on one thing in life. You become very good at one specialty. You become an expert. In the process of becoming an expert you finely tune your whole being. You collect the important parts of yourself and you begin to live the life of a warrioress. You rid yourself of attitudes that are not essential to your task. If you believe in magic, you can learn to do wondrous and magical acts.

Ginevee
Crystal Woman

PALETTE OF LOVE

Love is something we all want. See your life as a canvas spread out before you upon which you can manifest any reality you want. You can paint a picture of anything you can imagine. But there is something you must know before you pick up the paintbrush. If love is absent from your palette, your picture will be just that: a picture. In order for it to come alive as an art form, to explode out of two flat dimensions into multidimensional existence, you must come from a place of love.

Lynn Andrews
Love and Power

MASTERY IS THE SECRET

"Mastery is a teaching here," Twin Dreamers said.
"You must be willing to go to the bottom. You
have to be willing to have badger dung thrown at
you for your mistakes. You have to be willing
to beg, to stand on some street corner and
sell your ability for nothing."

"What then?" I asked.

"Then, if you have the ability, people will find out
that you are really accomplished, that you have
learned mastery. They will sit down at your feet
and listen to what you have to say."

"What is the purpose of mastery?" I asked.

"A lot of people want mastery for different reasons. Perhaps they want money or a big airplane."

"But why you, Twin Dreamers? Why do you want mastery?"

She laughed. "I would say that I want mastery just to know if I can handle it."

Twin Dreamers and Lynn Andrews
Star Woman

BALANCE OF POWER

Women take their power as women when they go through the gateway of menopause, the gateway of wise blood. But when they take their power as women, true sacred power, they cannot forget the male aspect of that. They cannot forget that they are always working for balance.

Lynn Andrews

ONENESS OF LIFE

"To make a choice is to divide your power. In a sense, there is no choice ever; there is only a oneness of love in the universe." Jaguar Woman stood up, and taking a branch from a tree, she separated it from the trunk with a loud crack. "But even if you separate the branch from the tree, you have still not separated the oneness of all life from itself. You make a choice depending upon who you feel that you are in this world."

Jaguar Woman and Lynn Andrews
Dark Sister

MYTHOLOGY OF OUR MORTALITY

We create dramas. We create the characters in our lives so often. Many of us experience something like mythology when we go into the shadow side of ourselves as we face death or illness or loss. Unexpected changes mean so much in our preparation for the understanding of our mortality. They deepen us so we can find the hidden meanings in our pain and our longing.

Spider Woman
Tree of Dreams

MAGIC IS WHAT WE SEEK

Magic is part of the unknowable—that which you
cannot describe, but which exists and makes your
life extraordinary. It is part of the goodness of
your spirit. It is that mysterious and intriguing
part of your spiritual life. Magic is what
we are all looking for.

Lynn Andrews
The Power Deck

IRON WOMAN

Take time alone to reconsider your life path, to reconsider what it means to be woman. In shamanism, my teachers have taught me to see signs in the world that things do not happen by accident. I am now stopped on the freeway and I look in front of me at a license plate that says IRON TREE. I think, it is true isn't it? Women are made of iron. We are asked to be everything. We have always been asked to endure. And so we do!

Lynn Andrews
Woman at the Edge of Two Worlds

TAKE YOUR POWER

Understand the source of power. Power does
not come from wandering between this belief and
that in a dilettantish way. Power comes from an
extraordinary experience that you may have and
share. The power is in it because you have lived it.
Understand where power lives.

Lynn Andrews
Writing Spirit

CHERRY BLOSSOM WISDOM

"Yes, O Kiku, just as your own existence in the world, your goodness and your ability to search out the truth, your curiosity for the mysteries of life affect everyone around you, the cherry blossoms settling on the surface of the water affect the pond in every aspect. We think that if we initiate an action, a movement, a design in Tokyo, it probably won't affect anyone anywhere else. But somewhere in Chicago, somewhere in Paris, it is felt in some way. Energy goes out from us we know not where."

O Kiku and Lynn Andrews
Shakkai, Woman of the Sacred Garden

WE ARE MEDICINE WOMEN

It will be as I say.
Spirits, we greet you.
We have the powers to bind it, cut it, change it.
We have the medicine, the power.
We have the light.
We have the truth.
We are medicine women.
We conjure you to come forth.

Twin Dreamers
Star Woman

FIGHT FROM YOUR HEART

We must unite, all of us. Those who choose not to see but to destroy will reap the effects of their acts and will also be destroyed. It is the law of the time. People today have to fight to live. But a true warrioress fights from the heart, and that is what is forgotten. But the heart will be remembered.

Agnes Whistling Elk
Windhorse Woman

CROSSROADS OF TIME

Ruby looked at me and held out her hands. I felt her fingers with mine and the strength of her grip.

"It is time, my daughter. It is near dark, the time when the world changes and the mysteries of power walk the crossroads of the earth. Come, join us in ceremony."

Ruby Plenty Chiefs and Lynn Andrews
Woman at the Edge of Two Worlds

SEPTEMBER

GIVING BACK

Your connection to Mother Earth is important,
how you have honored and given away to her.
People of the spirit understand each other around
the world. The gods live in the sky. They speak the
same language. Power is in the rocks and the earth.
That means that when we take something from the
earth, our mother, we must return that energy in a
ceremony, with honor. Then the power stays happy
and never leaves. Power only leaves when you
take and never give back.

Ginevee
Crystal Woman

LOVE ALL OF LIFE

To love is to love all of life and all of the manifestations of life, because all of life is a manifestation of your creator, which lives within you and within all things.

Lynn Andrews
Love and Power

A HIGHER PLAN

It is in your spirit that you develop trust in yourself and your abilities, along with faith in the world around you that even though life may be fraught with difficulty today, the Great Spirit has a higher plan for you. All you have to do is stay true to the person you are in your spirit, the person you are in your body-mind at the center of your own existence, the place where you are one with the Great Spirit and all of life.

Lynn Andrews
Medicine Woman Visions, Online Course

DRAW YOUR LANCE

"Sometimes you just have to be born to something.
If you have the lineage of being the chief, the king,
a Medicine Woman, anything, then you must draw
your lance. And by that I mean you have to be
willing to do whatever it takes to be the
master of what you do."

"What do you mean by lineage,
Twin Dreamers?" I asked.

"I meant it as a twin sister. Lineage means courage.
Do you have what it takes? When you get scratched
time and time again by the thorny brambles, will
you go home crying or will you ultimately master
the art of berry picking and enjoy the rewards?
That's all."

Twin Dreamers and Lynn Andrews
Star Woman

LETTING GO

What happens in your body when you find joy? You let go of the resistance in your body, the shielding that is around your solar plexus, and you open your heart and you open your mind. You let go of judgment, criticism, and fear, and you move into your body-mind. You open up. You let everything relax and surrender to infinite trust.

Lynn Andrews
Protector of the Children Shield, Online Course

UNDERSTAND YOUR CREATIVE SOUL

"For the most part, people seem to need comfort
and distraction from any real confrontation with
the undercurrents in life. My life is my work of art.
I am a spiritual woman like you, an artist looking
always for my expression. But to See is much more
difficult than to express. To See the undercurrent
is to approach dreams and your subconscious with
open arms, allowing the subtle essence of your
existence to become visible. Feelings of fear and
anger are healed only by an understanding
of your creative soul."

Edna and Lynn Andrews
Tree of Dreams

DUALITY

When an artist creates a painting, she thinks about her painting. She intuits that painting. But then she has to go outside herself to create that work of art, and that creates a duality. When a poet creates her writing, she must write it on a piece of paper, and it exists separate from her even though she created it. In the creation of a piece of art is a kind of bliss that comes from the Great Spirit, from your god, whoever that may be. It is a feeling of inspiration and joy. It is the true art of inspiration that makes us happy. It is the state of oneness with all life that we are all searching for.

Lynn Andrews
Woman at the Edge of Two Worlds

SHAMAN PRAYER

In shaman prayer we pray not only to the Great
Spirit but also to Mother Earth and to the powers or guardians of place. If it is raining, we pray to
the rain as if it is a being in itself. It is something
we consider as having life; it is an energy form.
So prayer becomes an exchange of energy, a direct
communication with the rain, or the clouds, the
wind, thunder and lightning, calling in the spirits
of being that influence the weather.

Lynn Andrews

PROBLEMS AND SOLUTIONS

"You can change the location of evil. You can move it around, but you cannot make it disappear," Ginevee said.

"But there must be some way," I said.

"Understand, my daughter, any solution that you come up with will only give birth to a new problem. It is the way of evolution and the law of life."

Ginevee and Lynn Andrews
Crystal Woman

ENVISION WHAT YOU WANT

If you are someone who believes that you don't
have the possibility of having a happy, successful,
and healthy life, doing things that you love to do,
then you probably won't have a happy, successful, and healthy life doing things that you love
to do. But if you can change your mindset about
the possibilities that life holds for you, then you
can change what needs to be changed to alter the
dreary course of your life. You shape-shift.
You change your belief structure about your
own self-worth and you shape-shift from
a person who has no future into a person
with endless possibilities in life!

Lynn Andrews
Coming Full Circle

YOUR GREATEST TEACHER

If you want to live a rich and fulfilling life, make death your ally. If you are afraid of dying, you will also be afraid of living. Grief is sometimes the only gateway to higher levels of consciousness, and it is a hard taskmaster. But if you can look at grief as a teacher, you will grow.

Lynn Andrews
Sacred Vision Oracle Cards

LOVE IS ALL THERE IS

We are only transformed by the process of love. It's all we have, and it's all that we are. Without that, we have nothing and we are nothing.

Sin Corazón
Dark Sister

ARE YOU TRUE?

"How do you know when the spirits stand up?"
I asked.

"You may see their luminosity. We have called the good spirits, and they are beautiful. You may feel a slight pressure or a rustling touch. Now do with your bundle as I do with mine."

Twin Dreamers unwrapped a small bundle. She arranged the items in a select way, and I followed her, doing the same.

"Follow my song as best you can. Sing from your heart. The spirits want to hear your voice. They want to hear if you are true."

Twin Dreamers and Lynn Andrews
Star Woman

MY FUTURE IS BRIGHT

The alchemy of life is about transformation, about
nurturing the lead of your everyday existence into
the gold of inner balance and the mystical harmony
of your spiritual and physical being.

Lynn Andrews
Coming Full Circle

FIND YOUR GATEWAY

This ceremony is for you, Spirit Woman—as it is
for all women. The soul of the mountain has sent
you a gift. The gift lives beneath the avalanche of
blockage that prevails within all sentient beings at
this time. The mountain has sent you a sign. The
trail is impassable and yet it must be followed.
Your life has been thus. To reach the next level you
must find the gateway within your own being and
the trail will become available to you once again.
You wear the shield of trust and innocence on
your chest. Follow the shield into your heart
and be reborn.

Windhorse Woman
Windhorse Woman

SINK OR SWIM

Remember, this is a life about enlightenment.
It is not about happiness or unhappiness.
It is about learning.

Ruby Plenty Chiefs
Dark Sister

TRUE POWER IS LOVE

First let me explain what I mean by power. This is a word whose meaning has been twisted and changed over time. When we speak of power, many people become afraid or uncomfortable. They think of police and tax collectors and others having power over them. This is not what I mean by power. Power, in my way of thinking, is partly the understanding of the spiritual energy that flows through all beings. This understanding comes from what I call a pulling down of higher guidance into your life—a process of vertical acts of consciousness in which you ascend to the level of spirit and bringback its wisdom.

Lynn Andrews
Love and Power

LOVE ABOVE ALL

Agnes placed her hand over my heart and whispered to me. "People should not be afraid of death—we experience the growth it brings so many times in our life. When you are afraid, as you were of Red Dog, your spirit disconnects until you start to love yourself again. It's love that conquers death and fear."

Agnes Whistling Elk and Lynn Andrews
Tree of Dreams

WHY I GIVE MY BEST

As you move toward living up to your abilities, you discover that you are moving toward embracing change. That is when you step into the mystery of the unknown. Always remember this: it is in the Unknown that all of possibility resides. When you open yourself to the unknowable, to the unfamiliar, that is when the energy of what you are seeking to create flows into you and becomes part of you, as you become part of it. You step into the unknown simply by doing something you didn't think you could do.

Lynn Andrews
Coming Full Circle

SACRED BREATH

All of the breathing exercises we have done are aimed at transmuting the breath into spirit so that you may become one with the universal sacred breath, the breath of the womb. It is circular breathing which will give you the flexibility and the innocence of a newborn. It is as if you are drawing your breaths from the earth, breathing with your feet, with the soles of your feet, bringing the air up into your body and out, up the right side of your body and down the left side of your body, always in a circular motion. The ancients said that in womb breathing, the air should be inhaled and exhaled completely without thought of the nose or the mouth or the body, so that you become like a child, like the life of the fetus in the womb that breathes completely independently of its mother.

Shakkai and Lynn Andrews
Shakkai, Woman of the Sacred Garden

BALANCE

Whether you know it or not, you chose to come into this physical dimension to become enlightened and to learn its lessons. Many of us want to throw away these lessons. We do not want to understand the exchange of material things, because we consider that a non-spiritual pursuit, when in fact it is a great part of our spiritual lesson. We must learn in the physical dimension to give away to the physical world and bring spirit and harmony into daily commerce and everyday life. Bring awareness to your understanding of money and physical things. Bring the integrity of spirit into your business.

Lynn Andrews
The Power Deck

A TIME OF RECKONING

Autumn is the time of harvest and reckoning as
the leaves on the trees and plants begin to fall back
to earth to be absorbed and transformed. It is the
time when farmers harvest their crops and reap the
rewards of their labor, the time when the entire
community comes together. This is the time to reap
the rewards of what you have begun.

Lynn Andrews
Coming Full Circle

HEAR THE SONG OF FALLING LEAVES

As the leaves begin to drop from the tree in autumn a harmonic is created. The harmonic is different with every leaf that falls and different again for every tree. The Tree of Dreams is you and me. We are all a Tree of Dreams. We are filled with yearning, joy, and love. We are filled with the teachings that we have received and the experiences that we have had. Our branches are the different times of our lives. The leaves are the experiences—the colors, the textures, the aspects of the divine. As the leaves fall, the song can be heard, a new song that plays on the wind is communicated to other trees, if they are listening.

Face in the Water
Tree of Dreams

LAUGHTER IS A PRECIOUS GIFT

When you approach a challenge and are so consumed by the barriers to perception that you cannot feel the joy in your life, put the challenge on a sacred circle with you sitting in the center. Imagine yourself joyously doing the things that give you spontaneity and laughter in your life. Visualize yourself as the sacred clown and look at your world upside down, through the eyes of humor.

Lynn Andrews
Standing at the Crossroads of Upheaval,
Online Course

WISE UP

"I'm counting on you to wise up one of these days,
Lynn," Ruby said. "The path of knowledge stings
sometimes. It is not an effortless pursuit. Sometimes you get cut and bruised, or even broken. But
when you find yourself wounded, that is not the
time to feel guilty. The important thing is that you
don't punish yourself unnecessarily."

Ruby Plenty Chiefs and Lynn Andrews
Star Woman

SHARE YOUR GIFTS

One afternoon as I stood shivering in terror at having to speak in front of a large audience, Agnes said something to me that I have never forgotten.

"But, Lynn, you love to give gifts, don't you?"

"Yes," I replied.

"Well," she said, "you have received many gifts of learning from us, so when you approach an audience, look at it from a different place. You implode your energy when you become frightened. Think of moving that energy out, and think about giving those people a gift of your wisdom and understanding."

Agnes Whistling Elk and Lynn Andrews
Love and Power

THE GODDESS IS YOUR BODY

"Make an ally of Bone Woman," Agnes said. "She is the caretaker of your bones. Talk to her directly. Do ceremony with her. Light a candle for her. Go inside your bones with your consciousness and honor them for supporting you all these years. Your body is one of the greatest teachers of all."

Agnes Whistling Elk and Lynn Andrews
Woman at the Edge of Two Worlds

A MOST EXTRAORDINARY ALLY

Aging is an extraordinary ally. As you age, you
have developed your self-esteem. You have walked
through many gateways of initiation. As you grow
older, you become more aware of the balance in
nature, and your energies are not wasted on
youthful dilemmas. Your beauty becomes a
beauty of a different kind. You contain a wealth
of knowledge and you become a wise elder.
This all depends on your attitude.

Lynn Andrews
Writing Spirit

EXAMINE EVERYTHING CLOSELY

You can see a thousand things in action. You can know all about a huntress by the ways she builds a fire, just as you can know about a bird by the way it builds its nest. When you look at an object or a person of power, you can see how much of a center it has. A true power object has a center. You are drawn to these things and you don't even know why, just as the world will be drawn to you more and more as you begin to collect your power and stand in the center of your own circle.

Lynn Andrews
Woman at the Edge of Two Worlds Workbook

REINSTATE THE SACRED BALANCE

"Understand what healing is. You are in a war against the forces of ignorance and darkness. In becoming a shamaness you give your body to the ancestress of light. You say, 'Here, I dedicate my life to the process of transforming the shadows of existence.' With your special abilities you are able to shine light into the darkness."

Ginevee and Lynn Andrews
Crystal Woman

OCTOBER

GIVE THE GIFT OF EXPERIENCE

"Remember," Ruby said, picking up a stick and pointing it at me menacingly, "you never learn through hearing borrowed knowledge. It may sound good; it may even be intelligent, but when you speak to people about something that is not part of their own dream, part of their own experience, they can never own what you say. They can never make it part of their own world."

Ruby Plenty Chiefs and Lynn Andrews
Woman at the Edge of Two Worlds

LISTEN FROM YOUR HEART

"Agnes, you have said that I would always remember stories when I needed them. But what I miss in trying to remember these stories is the subtlety behind your words. I have always written what you have told me. I need to have those details, otherwise I can't breathe life into this process that you and I have always had together."

"Ah, that is truly the point, Lynn. The story is only one aspect. The listening is the most important part because of the swirl of the air, earth, water, and fire. How you listen to a story and what that story actually gives to you through the wind on your face and the light in your hair and the feel of the earth beneath your feet, all of that comes together in the sharing of any living information. You become aware. You can see life in all the named and nameless things."

Agnes Whistling Elk and Lynn Andrews
Tree of Dreams

SANCTUARY

There is a place within all of us that is unscarred
and true. To me, bliss is within that place and it is
also that place where beauty leads me. Beauty is
the guide to that inner sanctuary. Discover that
sanctuary within you and move into it at will.
It is there that you will find the delight of
the great gift that your life truly is.

Lynn Andrews
Coming Full Circle

CHANGE YOUR PERCEPTIONS

"Is losing everyone the only way to learn how to get over attachment?"

"No, you will give it up long before that, because you will see that you never had them," Ruby assured me. "Mostly, you are attached to things out of habit, and those habits are broken as reality changes, and reality changes through your own perceptions."

Ruby Plenty Chiefs and Lynn Andrews
Shakkai, Woman of the Sacred Garden

LUMINOUS LINES OF POSSIBILITY

"To link your open heart," Agnes placed her fist over her heart, "and the substance of life force energy," she pointed toward the setting sun, "you must create a bridge, a kind of energy line. You can see this bridge coming from your heart as a beautiful, radiant energy line that is luminous and shining like that sun. It extends from your heart to the creative force of life. You see that force like golden light moving through that line and filling your heart and your body with a sense of richly glowing fullness. But it is your gratefulness that creates this possibility. Remember, Lynn, it is the gratefulness that brings you closer to God. And it is the gratefulness that recognizes and thanks God and all of the forces of creative life for being there within you."

Agnes Whistling Elk and Lynn Andrews
Love and Power

CELEBRATE THE JOY

For there to be joy in this world, there must be sorrow, for it is the darkness that defines the light. We must look at the dark side and honor it for the teachings it has come to bring us, for that which you refuse to look at ends up controlling you. But you do not live in the dark side. You examine it and discover its lessons, and then you turn to the light. The Sisterhood of the Shields looks at pain and suffering as a gateway to discovering the lessons that will bring you, ultimately, to joy. Joy is happiness, or the God-light within us. Through personal spiritual activity, you discover the light that is within you and bring it to life.

Lynn Andrews
Protector of the Children Shield, Online Course

HOLD YOUR POWER

"Many years ago, Lynn, we talked about the difficulties of comparing yourself. Never compare yourself to another person. It's an impossibility, and yet, we do it day in and day out. When we reach the age of wise blood, the sacred gateway into the second half of our lives, as we call it, we forget the fact that there is no second half of our lives."

Agnes Whistling Elk and Lynn Andrews
Tree of Dreams

PASSAGES

We are, together, moving into a new dawn of
history on this earth. A heightened infusion of
awareness is occurring. Walk in the sacred circle of
life and move through the sacred plateaus of
feminine existence.

Lynn Andrews
Woman at the Edge of Two Worlds Workbook

KNOW THE SACREDNESS
OF MOTHER EARTH

Mother Earth is the womb for all that lives upon
her, and she has so much to teach us about the
harmonies and rhythms of life, if only we would
take the time to watch and listen.

Lynn Andrews
Hero of the Dream, Online Course

STOP AND SMELL THE ROSES

Take time to dream. Learn to breathe and see the
lesson that is right in front of you. We're in this
life to learn something, and we're here because we
have a blind spot that eludes us. Know there is
still room to grow, to develop and become
more of what you are.

Lynn Andrews
Love and Power

I CLAIM MY POWER

You can never really teach anyone about power and the magic of transformation with words. You must use experience. You can look into the eyes of a woman of power and see that she has years of truth ahead of you. If you open your heart, her eyes can quicken you like a river heading toward the rapids.

Lynn Andrews
Coming Full Circle

I CHOOSE MY DESTINY

It is not for us to judge, to know, or even perhaps to try to understand. We can only take responsibility for our own relationship with power.

Jaguar Woman
Shakkai, Woman of the Sacred Garden

SHARE THE STORIES

My beautiful shaman teacher, Twin Dreamers, told me that stories stalk you. I always thought stories came from me. We always think we own our ideas, when in actuality, we share our ideas. I share my ideas with others, and they share their ideas with me. We give thoughts and ideas away because they are part of the oneness of consciousness.

Lynn Andrews
Writing Spirit

YOU CAN LEAD A HORSE TO WATER

I have been taught how to See the energy in people.
I have been taught how to heal, how to hold up
mirrors for you, and if you have the courage
to look in those mirrors—and that's the trick—
you can change your life. I can provide an
environment for you to grow, but it is your
choice to grow.

Lynn Andrews
Woman at the Edge of Two Worlds

EXPRESS YOUR LOVE

You can feel and express love in many ways, not only to one special person, but through your love of God, your love of the soul of humanity, and your love of doing and giving.

Lynn Andrews
Love and Power

TRUST IN GOD

"Lynn, when you lose your idea of the world, you lose your world. But your ideas are not necessarily real. So often we hold on to an idea so as not to lose our dream," Twin Dreamers said.

"But you have to trust what you see."

"Yes, sometimes. But only if what you see is the Great Spirit. There is no world here where the sun rises and the sun sets. This light and shadow is actually the Great Spirit. There is only the Great Spirit."

Twin Dreamers and Lynn Andrews
Star Woman

I AM UNLIMITED

IT is in your spirit that you develop trust in yourself and your abilities, along with faith in the world around you that even though life may be fraught with difficulty today, the Great Spirit has a higher plan for you.

Lynn Andrews
Coming Full Circle

EXIST WITHIN YOUR OWN INDIVIDUALITY

When the shield carrier reaches the top of the mountain, she never seeks approval, because approval is based on doubt. Your strength and wisdom are celebrated in your unique ability to view the experience of life with new vision. Power lies in individuality and the ability to see yourself through your own eyes and not through the eyes of another.

Lynn Andrews
The Power Deck

BECOMING ENLIGHTENED

"Think of the light within you. Think of the radiance that you are, that we all are, and think of death, when your body lies down and goes back into the earth, into the sacred mountain.
What is left?"

"The light?" I replied.

"Yes, the light. It is never-ending, and it goes back to its source. That light is purely of the sacredness of life, and it goes back to God. It is the Great Spirit. You are the Great Spirit. And that's really all there is."

Shakkai and Lynn Andrews
Shakkai, Woman of the Sacred Garden

A ROADMAP FOR A HARMONIOUS LIFE

Living a life of conscious intent requires a strong foundation, one that is rooted deeply in your own personal truth and your faith, both in yourself and in the divine plan for your life. No matter how bleak a situation may seem, always remember this: the Great Spirit loves you more than you can ever imagine.

Lynn Andrews
Standing at the Crossroads of Upheaval,
Online Course

WHEN YOUR MOODS MAKE OWLS

Ginevee sat down across from me on my blanket, her hand on the talking stick. "Owls can be story-tellers. Owls can frighten people who don't know about the power of stories. That owl is telling you that a story is coming to visit you. Now you must tell that story."

Ginevee and Lynn Andrews
Crystal Woman

FOLLOW YOUR HEART

Most of humanity tries to huddle in secure domains. Yet there are always those few we call walkers on the edge, or rim. They are searching for a bridge that leads over the river. There are many bridges. Some of these are masked under the name of religion. Yoga is a bridge. Sufism is a bridge. In the end there is only one bridge to follow, and that is the bridge of love. That bridge is the singular way to span into the beyond. Ultimately that is the one that gets us all there. When you experience the unexpected and the unprecedented in your life, follow your heart. It's the one sure path that leads to safety.

Zoila
Star Woman

I AM ENERGY

Everything we see in life is made out of energy.
When you realize and accept this in a conscious
way—that no matter what is before you, it is all
about energy rather than form—then you begin to
realize just how completely your thoughts, which
are energy, give form to your energy body
and to your physical body.

Lynn Andrews
Coming Full Circle

I AM FULFILLED

You don't have to choose a dream of suffering or
war. You can choose a dream of well-being. You can
choose a dream of success. You can choose a dream
of health. Why would you do otherwise?

Lynn Andrews
Coming Full Circle

I AM IN MY OWN CIRCLE OF POWER

As a warrioress, you must first be able to climb onto your own plateau of centeredness before help comes. If you're scattered, the spirits scatter. Once you gather your forces and pray and honor your inward silence, all the life-giving forces of nature become curious and flock into your energy field.

Lynn Andrews
Crystal Woman

RELEASE ALL

On the path to power and enlightenment, there comes a time when you give up what you have accomplished, the mistakes you have made, and the goodness that you have created. You don't own them anymore.

Lynn Andrews
Dark Sister

THINK WITH YOUR BODY-MIND

What you see is not necessarily what you think you see. And who you are is not necessarily who you think you are. To understand that there is a world of spirit living right alongside of us, that there is so much more to life than what we see, is to prepare yourself for the curve balls that life throws us.

Agnes Whistling Elk
Tree of Dreams

FORGIVE

It is a fundamental truth that forgiveness must be reached for there to be real healing in your life. Focus on fixing what is yours to fix, asking for help when you need it and giving help wherever you can, and you trust that there is a greater plan for all of us that is beyond the limits of our own vision.

Lynn Andrews
Coming Full Circle

BEING A WORTHY OPPONENT

"How does competition relate to opposition?"
I asked.

"I just told you the world is pretty much the same everywhere. Competition is the ugly sister of opposition. In true opposition, there's nothing to gain or lose. You can only benefit. If you start to think that you and the opposition are mutually supportive, you can lose a lot. You can't depend on your opponent. You can only depend on yourself. No one is going to save you. A contrary, a heyoka, sees the world as opposition and learns not to separate the inward moon lodge from the outward sun lodge. You can't compete with anything."

Agnes Whistling Elk and Lynn Andrews
Medicine Woman

LOOSEN UP

Agnes reached over and shook me briskly.
"Loosen up," she said. "Your whole body is
trailing after your emotions."

I tried to sit more erect.

"Your emotions deform you, Lynn. It is not in the
medicine way to let this happen. It is not free. It is
not good. You must make your 'heava,' your spirit,
sit up and take notice. Let your 'heava' know you
are no longer going to tolerate it."

Agnes Whistling Elk and Lynn Andrews
Star Woman

DIVINE LIGHT

You are not meant to live in darkness but in the
light of your own integrity. Move with the flow
of life and let go of any sadness from your earlier
years. Be serene and at ease as the light begins
to define you.

Lynn Andrews
Sacred Vision Oracle Cards

NOVEMBER

A SACRED BEING

By the very existence of a great and evolved being, the world and the people who touch that being begin to change. Just by their proximity to that being people are altered and become more. Then if that being actively deals with the forces of the universe, wonders can occur.

Ginevee
Crystal Woman

BECOME RECEPTIVE TO YOUR PREY

Being a great swordsman is understanding that
the sword is the extension of your own arm and
body. The female blade is created and given power
by a swordsman's ability to build his integrity, his
wisdom, and his strength. That is done with receptivity to the earth's power. Receptivity allows you to
set aside your thinking and go swiftly to the heart
of your prey. Power is always the same, as truth is
always the same, and the source is always female.
If a swordsman does not understand the power of
woman, the power of the female, the receptivity
of life, the womb of life that exists between man
and woman, that swordsman or swordswoman
will not be very powerful. A swordsman
knows this with his intent.

Shakkai
Shakkai, Woman of the Sacred Garden

YOU ARE LOVE

Love is not separate from you. It is part of you.
You're made of that love; there is no separation.

Lynn Andrews
Dark Sister

WHAT IS YOUR MYTH?

"Each shaman has a secret. All of her energy comes from her myth. My myth is the image of the horse, which to me is freedom," Twin Dreamers said.

"Freedom?"

"Yes, there is freedom in the sound of the hooves carrying me through space and time and other dimensions of reality. When I become the horse, I am created from thunder and lightning. I reclaim the horse. I participate in that plane of sympathetic magic. I am the apocalyptic energy of the horse, of life and death. As the horse gallops, I too approach you as in the ceaseless movement of the ocean's waves."

Twin Dreamers and Lynn Andrews
Star Woman

SEEK YOUR HIGHER COUNSEL

Everything in this life is part of the teaching of spirit. If you come upon evil in your lifetime, you are filled with a longing for the end of that evil, for light, for something better. But oftentimes, when you see that evil, you don't know how to get rid of it. You don't know how to heal it, so you try to get out of its way, to move out of its influence into something better and more comfortable and peaceful.

Jaguar Woman
Dark Sister

LOVE YOURSELF

The only place you are ever going to find love of self is in the moment. In our lives these moments need to be strung together like beads in a necklace. You don't hold onto a moment of joy, a moment of peace. They come and they go, because change is inevitable. What you do is become receptive to the joy, receptive to the peace so that you take the feeling within you and absorb it into your consciousness. You let God in; you let the life force in. That life force is love. It is of the Great Spirit, and it is the most powerful force in the universe.

Lynn Andrews

DUALITY OF ART AND ARTIST

When you dance, the dance becomes the dancer,
the dancer becomes the dance. When you dance,
you become the living expression of your art.
There is a oneness that is created with your
source of inspiration. The source is life force,
the Great Spirit that animates you.

Lynn Andrews
Woman at the Edge of Two Worlds

USE YOUR ENERGY WISELY

You are like a battery. You save energy and you use energy every day. Use it wisely, so that when you come to difficulties and situations that require extra power, you will have it.

Lynn Andrews
Love and Power

MAGICAL JOURNEY

A warm wind lifted the corners of Agnes's scarf,
and I took a deep breath, breathing in the scent of
desert foliage.

"You see, there is no beginning of life and no end
of life. It's just an agreement that we make when
we come onto this earthwalk to experience the
mirrors of aging, the mirrors of different seasons
of life," Agnes said. "But it is a dream,
and it is an illusion."

Agnes Whistling Elk and Lynn Andrews
Tree of Dreams

APPLES AND ORANGES

Agnes picked up an orange in one hand and an apple in the other. Holding up her left hand with the orange, she said, "Lynn, this is you. You're an orange, and I am over here, an apple. I am Agnes. We cannot be compared to each other, because we are so vastly different."

"But we are both human. We are both part of this dream," I said.

"Yes, and this apple and this orange are both fruits, and part of this dream, but you still cannot compare them, because they manifest differently on this earth, as do each of us."

Agnes Whistling Elk and Lynn Andrews
Shakkai, Woman of the Sacred Garden

CENTERING

Never leave your center. Count your bad points as well as your good. What is good and what is bad are most often purely relative. If you sense a weakness within yourself, explore it. It may become the source of your greatest strength.

Lynn Andrews
The Power Deck

ALL ASPECTS OF YOUR LIFE
ARE SACRED

Go all the way into the experiences of your own life
and learn from them. The circumstances of your
life are the most powerful mirrors you will ever
find. Trust the pathway you are on.

Lynn Andrews
Spirit Dreaming, Online Course

I AM FREE TO CREATE

Realize the magnificence that you are and make that your focus. Then shape-shift yourself into the truly wonderful person you are meant to be.

Lynn Andrews
Coming Full Circle

WISDOM COMES THROUGH YOUR BREATH

Breath is spirit, and breath is the source of life.
Breathe as if you have become the earth,
as if you were carrying the womb of the
earth within yourself.

Shakkai
Shakkai, Woman of the Sacred Garden

WE ARE MADE FROM THE STARS

"Remember this," Agnes said. "Power is peace within. The Sisterhood in its collective vision has attained this inward peace while here on this sacred Mother Earth. We women are the guardians and protectors of our species. But our fate is in the stars. We are made out of stars. And to the stars we will one day return."

Agnes Whistling Elk
Star Woman

TRUST

Trust your abilities and self-worth. To hear and understand words is very simple; but speaking words is a great responsibility, because words have power in every syllable. Words present a powerful duality, containing the energy to create and to destroy. Stay true to your own sacred path.

Lynn Andrews
Sacred Vision Oracle Cards

GO WITH THE FLOW

Spiritual energy flows through all beings. The essence of power in its truest form is the spiritual energy that flows through all beings. The first lesson of power is that we are all alone. The final lesson of power is that we are all one. We are all one with the Great Spirit, even the rocks and the trees, the plants, the animals, all things of this world. We are all part of one another.

Lynn Andrews
Coming Full Circle

TOUCH YOUR DREAM

Go deep inside of your dream and your physicalness, because they are one and the same. They complement each other; they are opposite sides of the same coin. You stand in this life with a foot in the spiritual and a foot in the physical, which is also the dream that you create. Let yourself feel something about yourself that you have not felt before.

Lynn Andrews
Writing Spirit

AN ACT OF POWER

What is an act of power? An act of power is something that you manifest into the world from your own deepest passion. When you perform an act of power, you are manifesting your true destiny in life; you are living your dream.

Lynn Andrews
Spirit Dreaming, Online Course

LIFE FORCE IS READY TO BE BORN

"All living things eat other living things to survive. That is life, that is the nature of our dream," Ginevee said.

"That doesn't mean I have to like it. I just don't want to kill things. It's wrong."

"My wolf sister, it is not right or wrong; it is what is," Ginevee said. "When you take the life spirit of an animal or a plant, respect the power of that spirit. It is eating of the deities that makes you part of them. You are a mother goddess for that unborn spirit."

Ginevee and Lynn Andrews
Crystal Woman

LISTEN TO SPIRIT

If you listen to Mother Earth, she will teach you everything. Listen to spirit. The male spirit comes together with the female spirit of Mother Earth and they marry each other in the most beautiful of ways. This marriage is a dance within each of us.

Spider Woman
Tree of Dreams

LOVE IS UNCONDITIONAL

When you accept the unconditional love of the Great Spirit into the center of your being, you find self-love. This does not mean you are without flaws and vulnerabilities. The Great Spirit does not put conditions on love for us. We are the ones who put conditions on love. Know that we are part of the unconditional love of the Great Spirit.

Lynn Andrews
Getting Out of Spirit's Way, Article

BALANCE OF MASTERY

When we have achieved mastery in our lives, we transform our lives and our health into an experience of complete consciousness of who we are and why we have lived.

Lynn Andrews
Love and Power

DOLPHIN DREAMING

"I live in the split between the worlds, between the cracks of darkness and light," Dawn Woman said. "I carry the sun in my womb and give birth to it every dawn. I dwell in the seas of eternity where the dolphins swim forever. The dolphins live in the seas of the world. They impart their vast knowledge with great subtlety. The dolphins, who know the waterways as they know the blood of your bodies, will be with you. They are the keepers of the world's karma as surely as your karma lives in your blood."

Dawn Woman and Lynn Andrews
Crystal Woman

I FLOW FREELY

Change means letting go of what no longer serves
you, letting go of old fears and anger. Change
means letting go of the veils of ignorance that keep
you from seeing your own truth in life.

Lynn Andrews
Coming Full Circle

LEARN FROM YOUR DARK SIDE

It is so often in life that we learn from the opposite
side of the goddess or the god. It is that dark side
which possesses us, in a sense. That's our failing.
That's our weakness. And it is from that side that
we learn. It is from that side that we receive the
teachings that bring us to our wholeness.

Lynn Andrews
Shakkai, Woman of the Sacred Garden

I AM THE LIGHT

"I have often told you that your inside moon lodge is equivalent to your outside sun lodge. The moon is more powerful than the sun. In its passivity, it overwhelms the world and becomes only light."

Agnes Whistling Elk and Lynn Andrews
Star Woman

THE WISDOM IS SAFE

"Life is a planting of the spirit so that a body can be formed from the dying seed. The monsters you have seen are the bardos, or stages of life, that you have lived on this earth. Without this earth, the seeds of the spirit would have no place to be born. You are a keeper of this mother garden."

Windhorse Woman and Lynn Andrews
Windhorse Woman

HONOR THE ELDERS

"The elders," I said, "why does Red Dog want to take power from the elders?"

"Because they know the stories," Ruby said. "They know the stories that inhabit this world. Stories must be heard. Stories must be told. Your story, little one, is a different one. It's a different kind of story. Your stories are about your spiritual growth, but you have shared these stories with a world that is unfamiliar with them. You must translate. You have grown along with these stories and helped others to grow. You have helped others to see in the mirror of your experience. This is part of your song. You are working with the elders. You love the elders and you always have."

"Yes, don't get caught in the dream," I said. "That is one of the parts of this story that needs to be learned. As people grow old, they actually become more awake—they learn a new reality. Their consciousness is a magnificent bridge between that world and ours. Yet we ignore the elders and demean them because of the change in their physical appearance and ability. We must learn to see them differently."

Ruby Plenty Chiefs and Lynn Andrews
Tree of Dreams

CHANGING LODGES

"You are woman. You are like fire now—you reach for the wise goddess mother in the sky," Woman at the Edge of Two Worlds said to me. "She comes to you. She is you. Remember always who you are."

**Woman at the Edge of Two Worlds
and Lynn Andrews**
Woman at the Edge of Two Worlds

DECEMBER

FREEDOM

To become free and whole—to flourish—
in spirit, mind, and body takes education and an
understanding of our own weaknesses. If we don't
name and accept our flaws so that we can heal
them, we will never know the true meaning
and joy of this life.

Lynn Andrews
Sacred Vision Oracle Cards

TONE OF LOVE

"O Kiku, when you feel love for Kat-san, something happens inside you. Perhaps you do not know it on a conscious level, but your cells begin to dance. They move in a rhythm. Love is a very healing energy, and there is a reason for that. It is healing, because love picks up on a higher vibration or tone and brings your inner ecology up into a level where wholeness is possible. When you are in love, you become receptive to another human being. You open yourself to a merging of personalities and spirits. For that to happen, your vibration must be much higher."

Shakkai and O Kiku (Lynn Andrews)
Shakkai, Woman of the Sacred Garden

DEFINE YOUR WORLD

When you learn conscious dreaming, you move to a higher level of spirituality, a higher understanding of your own sacredness and the role which sacredness plays in your life. You learn to trust the messages as well as the messengers, the spirits of the ancestors and sacred beings that you meet who give you information that will help you in your daily life. You learn to walk with one foot planted firmly in the physical world and one foot in the world of spirit in order to become whole and healed within yourself.

Lynn Andrews
Coming Full Circle

YOUR THOUGHTS CREATE YOUR LIFE

Remember that we come here to heal ourselves in this earthwalk. It is not a place where we just come to be happy. We come to be fulfilled and learn and become whole and to become enlightened.

Lynn Andrews

YOUR MUSES SURROUND
YOU ALWAYS

We all live in each other's hearts, even after
"duende" walks in your footsteps long enough to
take your soul. Somehow the entropy, the energy
released after creating something, floats with the
creative spirits of the dead. But energy is never
static and it comes back to you one day like bees
laden with pollen to bring you messages of love
and inspiration from the faraway.

Lynn Andrews
Writing Spirit

TRANSMUTATION

Understand that evil is part of the life-force.
It is a kind of energy or vitality. It is part of
the pulse of life that needs to be transmuted.
Evil is energy in need of transformation.

Ginevee
Crystal Woman

FOLLOW THE PATH TO POWER

We are all pilgrims on the path to the unknown.
We sit in awe and wonder at the architecture of
power. Ripen the receptive void within you, like
a womb accepting a seed. Open yourself to the
unknowable, to what is unfamiliar to you,
so that the energy of what you need in
order to be whole can flow into you.

Lynn Andrews
The Power Deck

TIMELESSNESS

If you want to understand the timelessness of your existence, sit with a rock and meditate; go into its slow, steady vibration. That rock has perhaps been part of this earth for millions of years. It has witnessed things that our minds cannot even begin to fathom, and it will share the essence of these mysteries with you if you will open yourself to the oneness, instead of being closed off by your separation from that rock.

Lynn Andrews
Coming Full Circle

NURTURE LIFE

We, as women, share a common understanding of what is real and what is true for the nurturing of life, however that is done, for the nurturing of our own soul. I feel that we have a responsibility to live in a way that will strengthen our spirit in our life, so that if the world goes into more depression ecologically and economically, we will still be alive to teach. That is our responsibility, and that is why we work together to preserve the sacred and ancient way of woman.

Lynn Andrews
Woman at the Edge of Two Worlds

ENERGY IS NEVER STATIC

We go into the soil blindly. Often what germinates
us is beyond our intelligence. From the smallest
seed rises the mightiest tree.

Twin Dreamers
Star Woman

PERFECT MIRRORS

"Don't you know that we are all the same? Don't you realize that we are all perfect mirrors for each other? Your sadness is my sadness, your impatience is mine, and yet there is a passage of time in this relative world of ours, and I have quickened much beyond your years. There will come a time when you will understand with your heart and not just your mind. You won't buy into the dream of everyday life."

Agnes Whistling Elk and Lynn Andrews
Shakkai, Woman of the Sacred Garden

HAVE FAITH

The truth is within your own heart and your own soul. When you become lonely and you become afraid, all the answers you will ever need will be found within yourself. Do not look so frantically out into the world for the answers to your questions. Look within, and ask yourself, "Am I being faithful to my own truth?" Losing that faith is the only real sin against the Goddess Mother. We forget who we are in this world of illusion. And it is the one thing that we must forgive and cure.

Grandmother
The Woman of Wyrrd

IT IS SAFE TO LOOK WITHIN

Creativity is one of the most powerful forces of all. Creativity is the child of love. Love is the life force of the Great Spirit, and it is the most powerful force in all of existence. Creative energy comes when you tap into the life force which is of God.

Lynn Andrews
Coming Full Circle

THE LIGHT OF JOY

Joy is an offering. When you present the magnificence of your being to everyone who experiences you, when you shine the light of your joy, everyone around you is lifted and inspired. This is your offering.

Lynn Andrews
The Lodge of Joy, online course

THE STORY IS NOW

Twin Dreamers took a crystal, and reaching out, she placed it in the center of the circle. I could see that it reflected a strong beam of light into each of our eyes, and it forced me to blink. She said, "This crystal represents a dream. It's my dream for the future, which, of course, is the present."

Twin Dreamers and Lynn Andrews
Tree of Dreams

WARRIORS OF SPIRIT

"We are, all of us, warriors of the spirit. For some, the way of building power is to test one against another, over and over. You and I and Shakkai teach ourselves about power by pitting ourselves against ourselves. You, O Kiku, move toward illumination by testing yourself. You do not need to hurt someone to grow. You do not need an opponent. You have learned the way of light."

Kat-san and O Kiku (Lynn Andrews)
Shakkai, Woman of the Sacred Garden

LIVE WELL AND LOVE WELL

Loving others begins as a process of reaching across
the boundaries that separate people and opening
yourself to a true oneness of spirit where experience
is shared, where you meet kindred souls moving
through lives not so different from your own.
Once the gateways to all possibilities have opened,
your life will be filled with extraordinary
shifts and changes.

Lynn Andrews
Love and Power

TAPPING INTO POWER

Water is like power, just as power is like water.
It changes every day.

Julio
Dark Sister

RIDE THE FIRE

Ride the fire when it enters your body. Centuries ago woman held the power on earth. She knew the alchemy of heat would purify her body and change her forever into a being of power. The heat is the source of your new life. Some do not need the fire in their bodies. They can still ride me into the land of their dreams.

Woman at the Edge of Two Worlds
Woman at the Edge of Two Worlds

SPIRIT LIVES IN YOUR BONES

The bone-keeper doll represents your life. The
spirit lives in your bones. It holds your good inten-
tions, the things that you want to accomplish in
this lifetime. Your spiritual and earth-plane goals
are part of the body of the bone-keeper doll.

Agnes Whistling Elk
Star Woman

WINTER

Winter is the time when frigid temperatures send plants and animals alike deep into hibernation and dreaming in preparation for a new cycle to begin. Life is a circle that never ends.

Lynn Andrews
Coming Full Circle

SOUL RETRIEVAL

Symbolically or literally, we give away our power to
people. We give away the power of our understanding. As we experience difficulty in our lives, we
crystallize into something solid, rigid, unflowing,
and we lose what we have come here to find.
We have to understand it all, even things we don't
want to speak of, such as sudden illness and the
specter of mortality. These emotional crystalliza-
tions form the underlying core of what drives us
from one experience to another if we are fearful.
When we heal, we are transformed,
and the next time we come from love.

Lynn Andrews
Tree of Dreams

DREAM IT!

We use the word "dream" to explain the creations of our imagination, which we then look at as rather childish, even though everything that we do begins somewhere in our imagination. We use the word "dream" when we talk about our daydreams, which we so often consider to be those flights of fantasy that give us a brief respite from the pressures of our world, something that isn't real but is nonetheless a nice break from reality. I do believe, however, that the Wright Brothers would heartily disagree with you if you were to say to them that their daydreams were not real! Always remember this, if you can dream it, you can do it.

Lynn Andrews
Coming Full Circle

STORIES NEED A VOICE

This story is a part of your future life. People think that stories are outside of them, like truth and power. But they inhabit you like your own life-force and they animate your being.

Ginevee
Crystal Woman

CELEBRATE YOUR BIRTH

The Great Spirit asks you to celebrate your birth.
Celebrate this great opportunity that is your life,
this wonder that contains the mysteries of all that
has ever lived. You know everything, if only you
could access the ancient memory contained within
your subconscious mind in a celebration
to the Great Spirit.

Lynn Andrews
Woman at the Edge of Two Worlds Workbook

I AM A WORK OF ART

We are all in the circle. We all live on this earth;
we are all a part of this earth and the sky and the
waters, the fire and the air and the stones and
the mountains. As the first lesson of power says,
we are all alone just as a mountain stands alone
over the plains. And yet, the last lesson of power is
that we are all one, that in all of these elements,
all of this beingness there is a oneness and
we cannot be separate. For a work of art
to be whole, it has to have unity.

Lynn Andrews
Writing Spirit

YOU HAVE A LIFELINE

"During the climb up the butterfly tree, it was as if I were hanging onto an invisible cord," I said.

Agnes and Ruby nodded in satisfaction, looking at each other momentarily.

"That cord lives in your will," Agnes said. "The butterfly helped you sense it. You will learn how to throw it out ahead of you in times of danger and follow it to safety at the end."

Agnes Whistling Elk, Ruby Plenty Chiefs, and Lynn Andrews
Jaguar Woman

POWER IS IN THE WAITING

Power is held in the silences and the stillness. When you pull back a bow or compress a coiled spring, there is a moment of stillness before the release. Power is found in that moment. Whether pulling back the bow and aiming your arrow or using techniques in your everyday work, there is power in the waiting. The simple stance of considering and cultivating a tremendously heightened state of awareness allows you to gather great power.

Lynn Andrews
Love and Power

DECEMBER 29

SEEK YOUR INWARD SKY

"To shamanize someone, you look at what they can become, not just what they appear to be. Look at the magnificence of possibility in an individual. And then look at what they are, and you locate their pain, their tragedies, their incompleteness. This creates a space between what is and what could be. It is in that void that enlightenment exists. It is from here that we all come and must again return. That is where the stars live within you, the constellations. If you approach a person in the immeasurable void or emptiness and pour your intent into their constellations, you will move them. A shift begins to occur. The stars move and form anew. Pour the intent of your will and the attention of your mind into that place of inward sky, and you initiate their becoming."

Twin Dreamers and Lynn Andrews
Star Woman

TREE OF DREAMS

"The Tree of Dreams represents truth in your life. The Tree of Dreams is all that we are. When our leaves fall, they are golden and beautiful. They carpet the earth with memories of our lifetimes. Lie down in those leaves. Wrap yourself in the memory and grieve with your whole heart and soul, and then let your grief blow away, like leaves on the wind. Be done with it and never look back. For us, the Tree of Dreams was cut down, and we lost our way. Our trees no longer stand, but their roots are still in place beneath the earth. And now through the love in your heart, we live on and the Tree of Dreams lives again."

She Who Walked Before You and Lynn Andrews
Tree of Dreams

YOU WILL REMEMBER
THE GREAT DREAM

You entered into life through the veil of the Dream,
because your reason for being here must be kept
secret from you until you find your way home.
You don't know who you are, but one fine day you
will remember. The possibilities you dream of will
become your reality.

Lynn Andrews
The Power Deck

PERMISSIONS

I wish to thank the following publishers for permission to use materials from the following books:

ACKNOWLEDGMENTS

I would like to thank the magnificent Sisterhood of the Shields for sharing their wisdom. Kathy Duckworth for her wonderful editing and constant inspiring support. To Michael Hohl for helping me create a space in this physical world to do this work. Sue Denniston for her patience and love in creating the design of this new book. And to my agent Devra Ann Jacobs for always believing I have another book to bring forth.

I am filled with gratitude for all my apprentices, mentors, and for the extraordinary people in my organization who work tirelessly to maintain this creative framework which is the form of Lynn Andrews Productions.

ABOUT THE AUTHOR

Lynn Andrews is the *New York Times* and internationally bestselling author of twenty-one books and workbooks on the power and wisdom of increasing awareness and shamanism, the oldest form of healing on earth. Her teachings grow out of more than three decades of study and work with the Sisterhood of the Shields, a society of indigenous shaman women of very high degree on four different continents. Theirs are the teachings of sacred energy, shamanic healing, and the divine feminine, rooted in Mother Earth and balanced around the four directions of the sacred wheel as they have been developed, studied, and handed down from shaman to apprentice, mother to daughter, in an unbroken chain for millenniums.

I would love to hear from my readers and your thoughts!

Visit my website for further information about my upcoming events the Shaman Mystery School and specials. Be sure to sign up for my free In Spirit Newsletter. https://LynnAndrews.com

For other inquiries contact my administrative office:

Lynn Andrews Production
P.O. Box 7736
Cave Creek, AZ 85327

Be sure to follow me on Facebook at: https://www.facebook.com/LynnVAndrews Twitter, Pinterest and on LinkedIn.